HOW TO GET MOTIVATED AND STAY MOTIVATED

123 WAYS TO GET MOTIVATED AND STAY MOTIVATED

KEVIN A MACKENZIE

AUGUST 16, 2016
AMAZON.COM

TABLE OF CONTENTS

How to Get Motivated and STAY Motivated

21. Sink Your Battleship With the Weight of Your Own Ammunition

22. Call Everyone You Don't Like

23. Finish What You Start

24. Start Some Daily Habits

25. Cut Out Things That Lowers Your Sense of Self

26. Cut Out All Negative Things in Your Life

27. One More Thing and Then Just One More Thing

28. Do too Much Till They Hate You

29. Save the Easy for Later

30. Challenge Yourself Everyday

31. Do What Scares You

32. Do What Others Don't Want to Do

33. Competition is Not Healthy

34. Help Someone Each Day

35. Buy Premium Fuel

36. Exercise Each and Everyday

37. Don't Look in the Review Mirror

38. Keep the Very Best People Around You

39. Join a Power Group

40. Get Out of There

41. Get Massive Attention

42. Difficulties Are a Good Thing

43. Don't Wait, Do it Now

44. Always Go Above and Beyond

45. Smile From a Mile

46.   Put a Smile in Your Voice

47.   Early to Bed

48.   Workshops and Networking

49.   Look at Your Money

50.   Money Can't Buy Happiness

51.   Goals and Objectives

52.   Reward Yourself

53.   Decide Not to Be Bored

54.   Drink More Water

55.   Your Calendar Needs to Be Filled

56.   Picture What You Want

57.   Keep Track of Everything That is Important

58.   Be Irreplaceable

59.   Listen to Programs That Motivate You

60.   Listen to Music That Motivates You

61.   Everything is Possible

62.   If it Can't Be Done, Then Do it

63.   Time Management is For Rookies

64.   Contact People Who Can Change Your Life

65.   Invest in Your Life, Often

66.   Make Time for Your Family

67.   Introduce Yourself to Everyone

68.   Don't Watch News, Make it

69.   Quick! Have a Sense of Urgency

70.   Don't be Satisfied with Satisfaction

71.   Don't Ever Lower Your Goals and Targets

72.   Don't Compare Yourself to Any Monetary Item

How to Get Motivated and STAY Motivated

123 Ways to Get Motivated

ABOUT THE AUTHOR

Kevin MacKenzie is a father of two boys, husband, sales guru and self-proclaimed motivated nut. Originally from Montreal Canada, then raised and currently lives in the Toronto Canada area. He works in sales, sales consulting and motivational consulting and speaking. Kevin worked in retail sales for the first 10 years of his career and then went into outside sales and sales management for the next 20 years.

In his spare time, he enjoys spending time with his family and friends, reading, gardening, golf and helping others. Follow him on Twitter at @kevinamackenzie and reach him at www.123ways.com

DEDICATION

This book is dedicated to everyone that has helped me become the person I am today. First and foremost, my wife Daniela and my two boys Lucas and Joshua I would like to thank. Without you three I'm nothing. You have never met a more motivated person than a child in a toy aisle. They are motivated, inspired, driven, focused and become the best closer any sales person has seen. We can all learn so much from the average two or three year old child.

Over the last 30 years of customer service I have come across a number of people who have left a lasting impression on me so I would also wish to thank the many store owners, store managers, sales managers and senior sales representatives that mentored and inspired me along the way. These people helped me become the motivated person I am today. They are, in no particular order; Ron Orsatti, Mike Orsatti, Bill Darling, Mike Berlin, Howie Berlin, Dave Cowan, Brett Shepherd, Michael Prendergast and Tom Ferguson. Last but certainly not least I'd like to thank my parents Don and Vivian. Without your expert guidance and unconditional love, I would not have written a book like this or any other.

INTRODUCTION

I thank you for getting my book: How to Get Motivated - 123 Ways to Get Motivated and STAY Motivated but more importantly I want to congratulate you on your decision. You are already leaps and bounds over most of your friends, co-workers and neighbors. It takes a special person to buy a book about motivation and you are it.

So who needs to be motivated? Is it people in sales? Is it a school teacher? Perhaps the President of a large corporation, the Manager or the new rookie employee about to start their first day? Is it a young entrepreneur working out of their basement or garage? How about someone that is looking for a job because they've been unemployed for a while? A trades person? A Politician? A student or a stay at home Mom? I think you know the answer by now. Everyone! We can all use a boost from time to time. This book won't just help you get motivated but it will help you to stay motivated.

It is easier to get motivated than stay motivated, unfortunately it is even easier to get unmotivated or lazy or start slacking. Look at all the negativity there is on the television, the internet, a newspaper or even around the office water cooler. You can get depressed just watching the first five minutes of your local news cast but the trick is not to absorb that garbage but stay motivated and positive.

How do you stay super motivated? What gets you excited? What gets you up early in the morning and keeps you up late at night? If you didn't answer fast or you didn't answer at all or you only had one or two things, then you came to the right place. These pages contain exactly 123 things to get you motivated AND keep you motivated. It is as easy as 1-2-3.

When you do nothing, nothing happens. You need to start to make things happen so how are you going to do that if you sit on your butt all day? It's like a cashier who has an empty register. How will she make change without any coins? You need to fill your cash drawer with a lot of coins and small bills to make all the change necessary to profit from this book or any other book that helps you make change. Don't wish you had six pack abs if you aren't willing to do some sit-ups.

Everyone wants something to be different in their lives but most people are afraid of change. They are scared because it is the fear of the unknown. You will read more about fear and how to overcome it later in the book.

If you're not motivated, then nothing else matters does it? It doesn't matter how great your job is or your relationship is or how great the product is you are selling or how wonderful your students are. None of that matters if you aren't motivated to do something about it.

How to Get Motivated and STAY Motivated

What is motivation? It is that desire and push to do things. It keeps you excited and determined to get tasks done that you didn't think were possible. It will have friends and family asking you if you are on something. You can answer that you are drunk on life and overdosing on happiness. It will get your co-workers to ask you to turn it down some because you are making the rest of them to look bad. You can then answer them all: 'no way!'

Motivation isn't a one book one read thing it's like goals or targets. Most people think about a yearly goal January 1st and very quickly forget it because that's what everyone did at the beginning of the year but how much motivation will you get from thinking about it a couple of times and perhaps writing it down once? Now consider this, I write my goals down in the evening and when I wake up every day. Most of the time I'm writing about three to five goals each time. Now who do you think will stay more focused? That's over 700 times a year versus one just once. Considering it could be as many as five goals each time that's over 3500 goals a year! If you keep writing them down, you will stay more motivated to get them done.

You may have heard the comparison of motivation to bathing. Just because you did it today doesn't mean you don't need to do it tomorrow. You need to motivate yourself everyday by doing these rules at least once (preferably many) each and every day. Take in motivational books, audio and video programs, seminars, workshops, group and one-on-one sessions from me and many others.

123 Ways to Get Motivated

Now think about what you will learn in this book. If you take away just one or two things, I'd be impressed. You must refer back constantly and really remember them to help you in your personal and professional life. I would encourage you to get both the ebook, the paperback and audio versions. Sometimes you may want to write in the paperback, underline or highlight key points or favorite rules. Having the ebook version will allow you to have it on a mobile device to take when you travel or before a meeting or some other event that would require a little additional lift to power through. The audio version will help in times when you are exercising or commuting in your car or on the bus. That's what I do with my favorite books that help to inspire or help me in some way. I have more than one form of the books that I like and I hope the book helps you in more ways than you even know now.

B.O.O.S.T. Your Motivation

One technique I live by to boost my motivation and I have included in this book is B.O.O.S.T. It stands for **Be Obsessed, Optimistic and Stimulated** in order to **Transform**.

Being obsessed about everything you do in your life and to such a degree that people will take notice as soon as you flip the switch will in turn motivate and inspire you. It will likely inspire others as well. Don't save the obsessed for big things. Be obsessed and driven at everything. You must be obsessed in all areas of your life in order to be motivated to the 100th power. I talk about all of these techniques as we go into the various 123 ways to get motivated. I don't always point them out in each one but B.O.O.S.T. is there every step of the way.

You need and must be optimistic and positive plus you must eliminate as much negativity in your life. Once you eliminate it you will be much more optimistic. An attitude of there is always sunshine even after the worst of storms.

Be stimulated by others and interested in their lives is just as important as being stimulated and interested in your own life and your life's goals. You also avoid boredom when you are stimulated. Boredom leads to laziness and then being unmotivated is just around the corner. You must be both interested (in others) and interesting (to others). Stimulate your mind and your body for instant and lasting change.

You will be transformed if you follow this root principle and the 123 steps. Your motivational transformation will have others inspired by your actions and your good character.

W.A.K.E.U.P. YOURSELF

My second technique is called W.A.K.E.U.P. You will wake up once you learn and adopt these principles. Again, these are peppered throughout the book.

Your **W**illingness to let go of the past will free you to have an **A**ppreciation of everything and everyone. In this book and others, you will gain the **K**nowledge to change the areas of your life that are necessary for increased motivation. You must be **E**mpowered to do it (get motivated) everyday, no exception. Finally, you need to stay **U**nbelievably **P**ositive.

It is important you don't let the weight of the past sink your motivational boat. Let go of it and allow yourself to move forward to positive change.

Having an enormous amount of gratitude for everything around you and everyone in your life and even having gratitude for people you encounter each day that you will likely never see again. Appreciate them. When you're appreciating more you prevent your motivation from depreciating.

Gain knowledge using all the tips in this book and others so you can get motivated but more importantly, to stay motivated for life. Every single day you need to wake up and get motivated just as you wood when you shower every day. Even if you wake up and you already feel motivated it's important to keep the momentum going and do it over again.

Get empowered and feel like you can do anything in your life. No goal is too high. The only limit to achieving your goals is the size of your dreams that inspired you in the first place.

Be so positive. Be so unbelievably positive. Having an optimistic outlook will increase your motivation because you always see the silver linings in life's dark clouds. Trust the situation and yourself that it will all work out in the end.

How to Get Motivated and STAY Motivated

1. SUCCESS SHOULD BE #1 ON YOUR TO-DO LIST

Many people might jump to the conclusion that I'm talking about money here. It can defiantly mean money and being successful at bringing in money but I'm also talking about being successful at your marriage or your relationship with your parents or your friends. How about being more successful at your job? There are countless things to be successful at, what are yours? What is important for you?

Success can mean many things to many people. However, we all need to tie that success to higher purpose. Now I'm not talking about religion but if you want to be so successful that as a result you paid for a new roof at your place of worship then that's great, go for it! I'm also talking about being successful at your marriage and falling in love with your partner deeper every day. Being more successful at your job might mean more money, a promotion and ultimately you will train and motivate the new generation of employees to do the same and that's what might inspire you but it is key to tie your success to something else because it will be that other thing that will motivate you.

Stop wishing for it. Being unsuccessful is not an option. You need to link your success to your moral responsibility, not a financial one and be focused on it like your life depended on it and you will be successful beyond your expectations and your dreams

2. LEAVE THE PAST THERE

Leave your unmotivated past behind you. If there is anything that you dwell on that leaves you un-inspired then leave it there, in the past. All your past defeats and failures should be left there. No rearview mirror in this vehicle called motivation.

If you wish to use past successes to motivate you, by all means, go for it. It is highly recommended that you do. We will talk about using past successes later in the book.

When you keep thinking of your past accomplishments that didn't meet your expectations then you take the wind out of your motivational sails. You will always wonder if you can do a task that might be similar to one that didn't work out in your favor.

Thinking of something negative from the past can eat away at you without you even realizing it. High stress is attributed to ulcers, over eating, high blood pressure, heart attacks and suicide. Having additional or unnecessary stress can't just kill your motivation, it can literally kill you. Seek professional help if you aren't seeing progress from this book or help from friends or family.

If you can erase all reminders of that thing that causes you to remember it, the better. Delete the files from all your devices, shed the paper files and stop returning to the negative aspect of the particular memory. Instead, think of what you learned from it in order to grow from it and how you could do it differently.

3. MOTIVATION, THE ENGINE OF YOUR LIFE

Nothing else matters if you don't have the motivation. You might have all the education but you will be out of work until you get motivated to look for a job or even write a resume. You might be the best looking person in your city or even the most charismatic but you will be lonely without ever a date if you aren't motivated to find love. Motivation is the engine and determination is the fuel that moves your life forward.

If you lack this thing called motivation, then you need to find it with the help of this book and others. You need to continually read and listen to books and programs many more times, to get the full benefit. They say you only retain a small fraction of a two-hour movie you just saw. How do you expect to remember 123 ways to keep you motivated if you don't read it more than once or listen to it only once? Repetition is the Mother of skill and learning.

Once you fully understand how important motivation is you will be more focused and realize that nothing else in your life is worth doing unless you have motivation. This is why I included it as one of the 123 rules. It is the understanding that is the rule. Once you understand that motivation is the engine you can start to tune up that engine and make it race ready.

4. REACH UP FOR HELP

I'm not talking about religion here but if that will help you then I'm 100% for it and recommend it. By reaching up I mean to ask for help from people around you. It's good to reach down and help someone up that has fallen or needs a boost, everyone needs to do that. What I mean is to reach up for help.

Find someone that can mentor you that can give you some guidance and that you can look up to. Perhaps you need to look on the internet or local paper for someone in your community that is more successful than you and introduce yourself to them. Many people will want to help you. Now look for someone who is tremendously successful. You are looking for greatness because you want to be great and not just good. Ask them if you could have a coffee with them for 20-30 minutes once or twice a month. Make sure you let them do most of the talking and learn from them. Once you reach their success level go find someone else to be mentored by.

Another good example is to join a Mastermind group or other group that has a lot of motivated people. Another example might be to go to a meeting of your local chapter of BNI (Business Networkers International) where your will find many motivated entrepreneurs all working together to help each other out. BNI would only work if you had something to promote such as your own business. However, it is still great to go to a meeting one time as a guest. If you have nothing yourself to promote for yourself then promote a friend's small business or one you like to frequent.

5. AVOID ALL NEGATIVE MEDIA

As I mentioned in the introduction, if you are trying to get and stay motivated the last thing you need is to listen or watch anything negative such as negative advertisements, news via any media or political attack ads.

Many shows on the internet or television fall in this category as well such as reality television shows that often has people trying to backstab each other for the sake of ratings. Cut that stuff out of your life, you don't need it and it's filling your negative cup and that cup needs to be emptied.

So you have a routine of watching or reading the news at a certain time of the day, change that by reading, watching or listening to various motivational speakers to get pumped up. For those that get much of their news from social media then stop following most of the deliverers of bad news and follow people that will motivate you, pump you up and make you feel better. You can start with me and follow me on Twitter at @kevinamackenzie

6. SUGAR IS THE DEVIL

We all know the side effects. The crashing after you have that 2pm donut or that sluggish feeling after having your morning coffee or tea with three sugars in it or the after dinner cake or alcoholic drink that is filled with sugar. You know it's bad so cut it out or reduce it as much as possible. It kills your motivation, brings you down making you reach for it again after the crash. Be pumped up on life and not sugar. We will touch on this again when we talk about exercise.

It's not just the sugar either. You know the stuff that isn't good for you so reduce it as much as you can. I'm the last guy that should be preaching healthy choices but I have my indulgences from time to time. I know it would be almost impossible to remove it all but by making healthy choices and not reaching for the sugar bowl as often. It will help you in the long run.

To prevent some of those sugar crashes try increasing your fruit and vegetable intake and then watch your energy level start going up after just one week or so. I know you are probably thinking that you thought this was a book on motivation and not dieting but it is often all tied into each other. I will touch on it again a few times because it's that important.

If you want to lose weight, simply E.A.T. I came up with this technique by understanding one big problem related to weight gain. Once you get rid of the things that cause you to eat the bad stuff (not just sugar) you need to get rid of or drastically reduce the bad stuff.

E.A.T. stands for **E**liminate **A**ll **T**riggers. Just like when someone tries to quit smoking and they stop going to bars or casinos in the beginning to eliminate the trigger of wanting to smoke when they go there.

You know what your triggers are. Once you eliminate your triggers you can stop eating many of the unhealthy choices you make. If you always pick up a bag of chips, a chocolate bar and a can of soda every time you do to the gas station then pay at the pump or go to a full serve gas station and eliminate the trigger.

Start looking at other areas where you get triggered to eat unhealthy or over eat and recognize them as they come and take note. Write them down and remember them. Finally, eliminate the trigger and you will start to eliminate the added pounds.

7. AVOID PEOPLE WHO DON'T MOTIVATE YOU

Avoid the people who don't motivate you or always bring you down. You know who they are in your life. It's the person who never has anything nice to say about anything or anyone. You realize when they are talking bad about everyone so then who do you think they are talking about when they aren't around you? That's right, you! If you work with them or you can't avoid them all together then drastically limit their influence in your life.

Do these people avoid any and all responsibility? Don't try and change their mind because that seldom works and it usually ends in an argument. People always looking to do the bare minimum and constantly looking for an easy out or short cut should be limited in your life. You are looking for motivation and you won't find it with them.

Perhaps they are the reason you aren't motivated or at least could use some more. If you look at your closest friends but more specifically the ones that you speak with most often, what are they like? They are usually like you! Don't let these unmotivated "I'll do that next week" kind of person rub-off on you.

You will recognize these people when you hear their lack of inspired talk about shortcuts and workloads that seem much less than yours. As the expression goes misery loves company. So let misery be lonely and get as far away from the unmotivated as you possibly can.

8. AVOID PEOPLE WHO ARE ALWAYS NEGATIVE

Similar to the previous one but these people are always negative. Listen for them to say things like: That won't work. You can't change that. I smoke because nobody likes a quitter. I don't like that. I hate that. I hate that person...STOP! If you know someone like this avoid them like the plague because that's what they are, the plague.

Keep company with them and they will infect you with their virus of negativity. Negative people like to spread their negativity to others and have the people that listen to them jump on their bandwagon and join in. This is similar to the schoolyard bully who wants people to join in in his/her spew of hatred and get you close so you can be in their negative aura.

Again, like number seven, don't try to change them as it will likely not end well. Just walk away and keep walking. Perhaps the reason you are not very motivated, lack enthusiasm, aren't very positive about life or are even negative about it is because of the people you associate with. You must positively not have negativity around.

9. BE A FANATIC OF YOUR OWN LIFE AND CAREER

Be fanatical at your career, personal life and everything around you. Bring so much energy and passion to whatever you do at work, at home and everything in-between. There is a saying; fake it till you make it. It means be over the top until you are over the top. Be enthusiastic on every project big or small. It will get you in the right mindset and it will also be contagious to others around you.

Do this the next time you are alone in an elevator: wait for someone to get on with you. As they enter say hello to them in a load clear voice and ask them how their day is. Most people look at the floor or the numbers above the door in an elevator and would be surprised by your friendliness. However, it is extremely contagious and in most cases you will get a smile back and possibly some conversation. At the very least the elevator ride will feel quicker getting to your floor.

So everything you do in your day do it with a great deal of passion and energy and you will find your zest for life will increase so much that people will call you a fanatic.

The word "fan" as in "I'm a fan of that actor" is short for the word fanatic or fanatical. So be a fan of yourself because soon you will have your own fans because your appetite for life will be so ferocious it will be infectious.

Make a list of what you are absolutely fanatical about. It's different for everybody so take a moment to write it down. Thinking about it is one thing but once you write it down it becomes alive and active.

What gets you excited and drives you? What keeps you up at night with excitement? Whatever it is, write it down and keep looking at it every day. What drives you might not drive me but that's okay. What I'm passionate about might not be your thing either and that's fine. It's important you write it down because these are different than your goals.

You might be passionate about your place of worship and therefore want to make frequent larger donations than you ever could. If that's the case, then nothing can stop you from making more money or starting a new business if it meant you could do that. How do you think you would feel after you accomplished that? Would you feel more motivated to do it again or tie another goal to something else you are fanatical about?

10. IGNORE THE PEOPLE WHO SAY YOU CAN'T

When someone says you can't do it or it's impossible or don't bother or nobody has ever done it better or why try or you're going to fail, you need to just ignore them. Others will listen to that "advice" and give up but you're different because you will ignore that kind of person and stop listening to their nonsense and push through it all and succeed. I know you can.

They might have, in their mind, a sound reason for telling you this. Simply thank them for their input or suggestion and don't give what they are saying a second thought. They may have had a similar experience or know someone who tried and failed and what you are trying but those people aren't you and you are different.

Many school yard bullies have moved on after they don't get the reaction they were hoping for from their target if ignored. These people you are encountering aren't necessarily a bully but the end result is the same.

These people are trying to limit your possibilities, they are holding you back from your goal to making a better life for yourself and your family's life. They are likely not even doing it on purpose and that's probably even worse than if they were doing it on purpose. Simply ignore them and keep moving forward.

11. BE ENERGIZING

I've said it before sometimes you need to fake it till you make it. Be as energetic as possible. It's like exercise, you will get tired quicker in the beginning until that muscle keeps going (and growing) from the training. If you exercise once or twice a month what do you think will happen? You'll be tired and sore for a few days with almost zero results. If you train several times a week do you think you will see results? Of course! That's why it's important to constantly be energetic to build that muscle so it becomes a habit.

Be energizing even when you don't feel like it because that's the point. You will feel it all the time with practice. When you are energetic you feel more motivated and when you feel more motivated you feel more energetic!

Don't reach for alternative methods of energy like too much coffee, energy drinks, sugary snacks or over the counter/street drugs for 'pick me ups' in the day. These will lead to 'crashes' after the alternative method wears off. Go all natural. It's okay to be a little tired or cranky in the beginning but power through and soon you will have so much extra energy that the people around you will think you're on something.

We will talk about these things later in the book but you can get that extra energy from things such as exercise, vitamins, better quality food, regular sleep patterns and power naps.

12.   DON'T LIE TO YOURSELF OR ANYONE ELSE

You have to be honest with not only everyone around you but more importantly with yourself. So not even a white lie here when you ask yourself questions such as: What can I do? How can I do it? What is my potential in an hour, day or year? How can I help myself or other people?

It starts with you. Get honest with yourself when you hear yourself say "There is no time for that." or "I can't do that." My first job was in retail and I'd always hear excuses from late employees about their broken alarm clock, the late bus or the traffic. They were late because THEY were late. Take ownership if you're late or if you're wrong or if you come up short on one of your goals. Be honest and don't lie to yourself or others.

The people you interact with every day will also appreciate this. Here is a common mistake many people make without realizing it and I'm guilty of this one too.

When someone asks you a question that stumps you or you might have difficulty answering don't say something like "Great question!" This annoys the other person because if they asked the question it is important to them and they don't need your approval or validation of the question.

You likely said that to buy yourself two or three seconds to think about it. Try this instead; "Please allow me to think for a moment." The other person will appreciate this more because they know you are taking the time to come up with a thoughtful answer.

13.   BE GIGANTIC

Be big, then be bigger! You need to be huge in your space, whatever or wherever that space might be. You need to own it. If you are a school teacher be the teacher every kid wants. If you are in sales be a business partner to your clients, if you are a student or a stay at home Mom or Dad then own that space and be the very best you can be. Be the very best anyone can be in that space.

Be as big as you can be. Be gigantic in your workplace and at home. Everyone around you will take notice and that's a great thing because you will start to get attention and that will motivate you to do even more or expand this giganticness to other areas of your life.

Be huge in the actions you take. Be gigantic at work. Be huge at home with your family. Be the center of attention at parties, corporate events or networking events so you can expand your network of friends or business contacts. One of those people could be your next good friend, boss, business partner, client or even spouse.

When you start being gigantic in your actions you will also start being gigantic in your thoughts. Your creativity will also go up and this might start the process of the next big thing in your life, you just haven't thought of it yet.

14. SEE THE SUNRISE

Do you want to be motivated or super motivated? Be up before the sun is! This will motivate you knowing that you likely beat most, if not all, of your neighbors, co-workers and, if you're in business, the competition too. You will get more done than they can before they rub their eyes or have their coffee.

Go to bed at 9 or 10 pm at the latest. Chances are you only need 6-7 hours of sleep. Now after seven hours of good rest it is now 4am. You will now have up to a four-hour head start than the rest of the people in your city. You looking for a promotion at work? Start showing up one or two hours early and watch what happens! Looking to get a hold of that hard to reach client? How about you be waiting for him or her when they arrive at their office?

Want to read more books? Want to write a book? Never had time to take an online course? Not enough time in the day to start exercising? Try doing some or all of these things just after your new wake up time! It's about getting more done so you can get more accomplished.

Get a head start on life and your morning. While everyone is sleeping you have worked out, showered, had breakfast, written your goals down and started your day. So how do you do this?

Chances are if you are awake after 9pm you're just watching that garbage on television that we discussed or doing something else that won't motivate you like eating a sugary treat or salty snack. Go to bed early and wake up early it's as simple as that!

Like anything new don't give up because you are doing the head nod before lunch. With some practice and perseverance, you will overcome it and get more energy as a result.

15. BE RELIABLE

Be reliable to everyone around you. Be the one that everyone can count on. If it's something hard to do and you are known as the go to person, then that will motivate you to do more and be more reliable and dependable. Have people be able to set their clocks by you because you are just that dependable. Now I'm not talking about if people find you predictable per say, I'm talking about how much people can count on you.

This will raise the confidence you have in yourself and if there had been any doubting yourself you will change your mind very quickly when you see so many people believing in you. When people are dependent on you it will become another foundation for you to build your motivation on. That's because these people count on you and therefore your sense of self-worth will be catapulted to new heights never seen before by you.

When people say they can trust you, that you are their go to guy or girl for many things that will fuel your passion for helping others and life in general. It's only natural to feel fantastic if you help someone and it will be a domino effect as the more people you help the more people will ask you for help and the more you will want to help.

Take a moment and write down how you can be more reliable

and this will actually boost your motivation and you'll be looking for areas where you can be even more reliable than before.

16. HAVE MORALS

Now this isn't when you find an umbrella you take it to the lost and found or that you went to a place of worship a couple times a year. This is about helping people, doing your job better than anyone else, providing for your family, finishing what you started and doing what is right each and every day. You have to be honest with your friends and family but just as important you have to be honest with yourself.

This means not making excuses to yourself for not hitting your goals or keeping your promises to yourself. So cut out the "I was a little under the weather today" or "It's not my fault because xyz happened". Don't play the blame game with anyone else or especially yourself. If you take responsibility for your actions, then it will truly motivate you to push yourself more and persevere.

When you live up to high standards and ethics this will change the way others look at you and think of you. However, beyond that the more important opinion is the one from the person who greets you in the mirror.

You will become a role model to other people when they see just how many morals you have and thus just how ethical you are. When that happens there is nothing that can stop this motivational rocket from taking off.

17.   DRESS FOR YOUR SUCCESS

You have heard the expression and it's so very true. When you dress up what does it do to you? Makes you feel fantastic! Not in a "Wow look at me!" vain kind of way but it will boost your convenience and motivate you. If you have a work from home job or if you are out of work and looking for a new job and you strive to be successful, then dress the part. Dress every day like you're going on that job interview or an important meeting with your company's President. This will get you in a work mode like nothing else and motivate you to be more professional on the phone calls, in emails and in overall work you do.

Save the jammies and slippers for Saturday morning cartoons with your kids. The rest of the week be professional. Even if you are heading to the corner store you need to look presentable because you never know who you will meet. Have you ever regretted running into someone because of what you were wearing or your hair hadn't seen a brush yet that day? Don't have regrets. Dress for success every day.

Other people will take notice and know that you always mean business. Don't buy into dress down day or casual Friday because it will bring down your professionalism, your creativity and more importantly your motivation.

18.   FAIL AT FAILURE

Failure is highly unlikely. Know that it's possible but it's so close to zero for you. Know that the one failure you will have is failure itself.

Think about the number of times in your life that you stopped doing something, you gave up, you quit. All those times are the ONLY times that you have failed. When you keep trying but you missed your mark or you didn't succeed then you didn't fail because you never gave up. Once you give in or give up on the task or your dream, then you do fail and I mean miserably.

Every set back is a learning experience that you can take something from. The next time you have a failure, you must first call it a setback or a learning experience. In the world of 'epic fail' videos people share think about what it does to a person's ego or feeling of self-worth if what they get labeled as a failure.

Imagine if you were teaching your child to ride their bike and they fell in a few feet after you let go. Would you call a failure? I doubt that. You would say try again. You might say don't worry about that, you'll do it this time. Think of that child the next time you have a setback. No matter what it was.

If you approach failure that way, then you will always succeed and you'll win every time. Fail at failure. Be a failure at failure.

19. BE A SUPERSTAR IN YOUR UNIVERSE

Strive to become the go to person in your universe. Whatever your area of expertise is, go with it and become a know-it-all. Soon people will seek you out for advice, they might ask you to write an article for a blog or better yet why don't you start that blog yourself? Perhaps you will write a book on the topic and then watch what happens when you add author to your title on the topic. Perhaps becoming a consultant or keynote speaker on your preferred subject.

We talked about you becoming the most reliable person earlier, now we are talking about kicking it up a few notches and become the superstar. Be so big that it will propel you into outer space because everyone wants your advice. This will cause your self-confidence to be on the top of the world with you.

Be giant in all of your actions, your beliefs, when you walk down the street or into be interviewed for a job or do a presentation. Decide today that you are a giant. Know that you are a Superstar. Say out loud right now: "Look out world because here I come!" Good for you if you actually did it. If you didn't, do it! If you still didn't, how much do you want change? How much do you want to be motivated?

20.   CHUNK YOUR LIFE

Break your entire life in different chunks. Your relationships (family, friends and business), assets (money, investments, mortgage/rent, etc.), work, special projects, vacation (travel), hobbies, learning and your sense of wellbeing (eating healthy, exercise or sleep schedule) or anything else of importance and become motivated about each and every one using the tips in this book. Once you get motivated and reach your goal in each area move on to the next one.

If you chunk it, you won't flunk it! You will find it easier to measure and achieve your goal in each one and it won't seem such an impossible task. There is no right or wrong number of chunks to have. Only you can answer that. Big chunks, small chunks, three chunks or 30 chunks it doesn't matter. It's like paying off credit card debt. It doesn't matter if you start with the largest or smallest balance or the one with the highest interest rate, it matters that you started.

These are portions of your life that you are chunking. Later, you will learn how to chunk portions of your day.

21. SINK YOUR BATTLESHIP WITH THE WEIGHT OF YOUR OWN AMMUNITION

Go into every project, every scenario and every aspect of your life with so much ammunition and fuel that you couldn't possibly lose the fight or even the war. It's about being prepared for what life throws at you.

It's like the boxer who builds up his stamina so he can fight 20 or more rounds so that when it counts, his tank won't be empty after seven rounds or 15. What's the first thing you do before a long car ride? Fill up your tank, right?

Always be prepared and ready for the next task or the next thing that life throws your way. Having the maximum amount of energy and positivity each day is just two examples of the various types of ammunition.

22.   CALL EVERYONE YOU DON'T LIKE

I'll talk in a few different chapters about doing the hard things first. It's procrastination you want out of your life. Putting things off never accomplishes anything good. Sure you feel great in the moment because you put off an important decision but how long will that great feeling last? Not very long at all! Are you still going to have to make that decision or do that task? Of course! So why are putting it off?

So call that problem client, that hard to get along with co-worker, that neighbor you don't click with or that family member you haven't spoken to because of something stupid or worse, something you don't even remember. I never said this journey will be all easy. In my opinion this is likely the hardest one in the book.

There are some easy parts but there are some difficult ones too. This part of your life has likely eaten at you and caused a lot of unnecessary pain. Get past it so you can move on and be motivated even more.

When you're done contacting all the people you didn't want to contact then you will have tremendous motivation to strengthen the relationships that are already good in your life. Then seek out new and fresh relationships in the form of new friends and perhaps new contacts if you're in sales or have a your own business.

23. FINISH WHAT YOU START

You've likely heard this when you were a kid from your parents or teacher but it's just as important now. When you have a lot of loose ends or unfinished tasks and business then it will keep eating at you. We trade off that task for a better feeling like watching TV then as the deadline for that task gets closer and there is a moment where you decide not having it done will be of greater pain to you than the pleasure of not doing it to do something else. Don't put it off another moment.

When something needs to be done for next week start today and see if you can finish it today. It will motivate you to do more and it will cause your friends and co-workers to know they can depend on you for anything.

If you want to feel unmotivated and overwhelmed, then have a bunch of unfinished tasks. The more you have the more unmotivated you will feel. Finish what you started so you can start to be finished.

All this finishing what you started will give you a great sense of accomplishment in your life. No matter how mundane or how challenging it is, get it done. It can start with this book. Most people that buy "self-help" books never finish them. Read this book within a few days at the most and you will be on your way.

24.   START SOME DAILY HABITS

Start some daily habits that constantly remind you that you are the one controlling your life and not any outside influences or people. Perhaps it's something to start the day like writing your goals down, prayer, a work out or a run. Perhaps mid-day is better for a daily habit such as meditation, a short nap or reading something for personal growth. Finally, you may also want to save it until after work or in the evening such as cleaning a different part of the house or having quiet time with your spouse.

Whatever your daily habit is, make sure you keep doing it every day for those few moments for yourself so you can continue to power through your day. This again will motivate you to do more and continue the domino effect and motivate you yet again. This is very powerful and will give you sense of control where before you felt like you were spinning out of control.

Finally, even though it will be a daily habit you still need to write it in your planner. This will strengthen the importance of that particular daily habit. If it becomes a habit that you do without fail, like brushing your teeth, you need to still put it in your motivated planner.

25. CUT OUT THINGS THAT LOWERS YOUR SENSE OF SELF

Having a sense of self or self-esteem plays a significant role in your self-help journey and your quest for more motivation.

If it isn't good (or good for you) then cut it out. We talked about sugar already but this is more than one thing. If it's smoking or drinking in excess then cut it out. It can be anything. If you don't feel good after doing it or feel guilty after doing it, stop doing it!

It doesn't matter what it is, if it doesn't feel good after you do it or part of you feels bad while you'll doing it then just cut it out. It could be drugs, eating too much or not eating enough. Don't participate in anything negative or something that lowers the self-esteem of another person. Cut out the negative behavior or even the negative thoughts because they are both bad for you.

Your self-esteem and your motivation go hand in hand most of the time. If your self-esteem is increased, then so will your self-esteem. Think about when you were in school and a bully made fun of your love of tennis. He lowered your sense of self in that area and he lowered your motivation likely overall but more specifically in that area. You would probably loose motivation to join the tennis club or even watch a game.

Simple rule and easy to follow. Don't do anything that could lower your confidence.

26. CUT OUT ALL NEGATIVE THINGS IN YOUR LIFE

You just learned about cutting out the negative behavior in the previous rule. Now you will learn you need to cut off all negative things in your life. Period.

The negative people will suck the life, joy and happiness out of you and out of the room they are in if you allow it. Cut them out of your life. Don't try and change their behavior because it likely won't work anyway or it may turn into a bug disagreement between you.

Write down anyone or anything in your life that brings nothing but negative thoughts and actions to your life. You know who and what they are so write them down so you see their name. Now cross the people out of your life or at least drastically reduce them if you really must have them around. Keep them always at an arm's length and take what they say with a grain of salt, as the expression goes. Keep only positive people and things or the 'can-doers' in your circle of friends, family and co-workers. Remove the rest.

Negative people can also affect you just as much as positive people can but you only want one group around you. Negative people are like a virus or some bad bacteria that just keeps growing. You don't need them.

We will talk later about keeping only positive people around you or joining different clubs and networking groups that breed positivity. So then why go to all the effort but still have that one friend that brings you down all the time when you are around them? It doesn't make sense.

27. ONE MORE THING AND THEN JUST ONE MORE THING

Have you ever gone to the gym with a friend that tries to motivate you to try again with additional five pounds or one more set or one more rep or two more laps? Those people try to push you and motivate you. They want you to see the potential in you that they see in you. Those people you want in your life and more of them.

That is the way you need to treat each and every day. Do just a little more each day. Read one extra page or chapter, help one extra person, donate that extra few dollars or drink that extra bottle of water. Become an athlete of your own life. Keep training every day in everything you do.

Each day you can add a little to every aspect of your life the more motivated and the more fulfilled you will feel. Look back on your calendar yesterday and see what you can add to it today and add to tomorrow and so on.

This rule, if followed to the letter might have you doing just one more thing for infinity but you get my point. Do just a little more when you thought that you couldn't do any more. If gives you an incredible amount of motivating power. Keep pushing so you can do just one more thing.

How to Get Motivated and STAY Motivated

28.   DO TOO MUCH TILL THEY HATE YOU

Increase your activity level so much that I want your day packed so tight that your calendar is going to bust at the seams. Whatever goal you have there should also be one that people will start to hate you. Perhaps hate is a little strong but I used it to prove a point and grab your attention. You definitely want some criticism or resentment because you are doing what they think is way beyond the norm and isn't humanly possible.

You will easily get more motivation from this because it's a form of praise in my mind. Other people are scared of you because they feel you'll get the raise or the promotion before they do or worse they'll be fired because you become the gold standard that all other employees are compared to. They will be scared because you are getting all the attention due to the fact that you are the go to person who solves problems.

You are doing too much, stop and smell the roses or take a break. These are just three examples of what you will hear. By now you know what to do right? Ignore them and do more. Who do you need to motivate first, you or them?

Think about all various tasks that you do every day. Try and put a number on them such as; How many emails do you send out? How much of the house do you clean at a time? You may also think about and write down; How many reports or presentations do you do in a month How much money do you make in a year? Now start to figure out just how you can do a little more tomorrow, this month or this year to increase each of those numbers and other things that are important to you.

This day and age where we have fast food, convenient this, less effort that it makes everyone wants everything with as much minimal effort as possible. We are in the convenience generation. It's where everyone is looking for a shortcut or a 'life hack' to do less and get more. That's why you will be criticized for not only doing more but wanting to do more because ultimately it motivates you and it helps you get to your goals faster.

Don't be confused with things that save you time. I don't want you washing your clothes in a stream and beating them against a rock. Look to do more tasks, help more people, smile more, be more motivated and happier.

29. SAVE THE EASY FOR LATER

Most people want to do the easy things first. Let's suppose that it's moving day and the truck is here. Do you go get your tooth brush or the toaster first? No, you get the bed, the sofa or that big armoire to load in the truck? That's right, you go for the big stuff, the awkward and the heavy stuff first. That's what you need to do in your life. When things need to get done grab the big ones first. This will give you tremendous motivation to tackle the rest and to tackle even more.

The things that you dread doing, you put off until the last minute, the things you avoid doing are the things that you need to do first. If you have a list of 50 things that need doing and one or two are the type that you leave to the end or avoid altogether then they need to be done first. Why? It will give you a boost on the other 48. The other 48 will seem like a piece of cake. Stop looking for the piece of cake and look for the entire bakery first.

This is much more motivating for you rather than doing 48 easier tasks and then still needing to do the two difficult ones when you might be more tired after doing the mundane 48 others. What three things feeds off of procrastination? It's time, negativity and laziness! Don't feed them, starve them and do what needs to be done.

Finally, take out your calendar or planner for today. Highlight the one or two hardest ones and do them first and then watch your productivity go through the roof.

30.   CHALLENGE YOURSELF EVERYDAY

It's good to feel challenged. It stimulates you, it makes you want to do more, you end up looking for more challenges and you get more motivated after each one you do. You want challenges in your day. You don't need a boring day; you need a doing day. You have to stop doing the things that don't challenge you.

Do things that make you feel uncomfortable. Go talk to your boss today, ask that person out you've had your eye on, write that book you have always wanted to do, start exercising or whatever it is that will challenge you, start being challenged and getting pushed beyond your comfort zone.

When you get to work do the hardest things first. When you have a weekend to do list, do the most difficult things first. Don't always look for the easy way or the shortcut. Rediscover life by constantly being challenged and stimulated every day.

By constantly being challenged both mentally and physically in the day you will be more stimulated and look for other challenges. You will want problems to come find you because it brings variety and helps you solve things for yourself or others. By doing the easy things first it often causes problems and then you run out of time to do the really important stuff. You then end up moving the task to the next day. Do that and you will start the procrastination process. Don't start procrastination, start action! Look for a problem today.

31. DO WHAT SCARES YOU

Do the things that completely scare the sh*t out of you. Sorry to be a little crass there but I really needed to grab your attention because this is that important. Think about different things that scare you and by doing them they will improve your life such as getting a raise, getting a promotion, meeting the love of your life, starting a new career, starting a business, starting a family, taking a trip or moving.

All those things above mean you might have to do something that scares you like talking with your boss about something uncomfortable, getting yourself out there and approaching strangers, going back to school, getting financing, having your first child, getting on a plane or totally getting out of your comfort zone.

It's said the word fear is an acronym for False Evidence (or Events) Appearing Real, meaning much of what we are scared of never actually ever happens to us. Imagine how much your life would change for the better if you did some of the things that scare you. Imagine how much more motivation and self-confidence you will have after you do the things that scare you.

Are you scared of heights? Good, go parachuting! Are you afraid of public speaking? Good, go do a talk at your kid's school!

Whatever it is that you are fearful of, go do it. Write a list now of what really scares you and then start doing each one. This will give you courage beyond anything you have tried before and trust me it will motivate you to do more things that would usually scare you and each one will be easier than the next.

32. DO WHAT OTHERS DON'T WANT TO DO

Let's assume you are looking for a new job. Everyone sends a resume, many will send a cover letter and a few might send a follow up email. However, how many will phone the hiring manager or the manager/supervisor of the position? Who will drop by the company and ask to see the person who makes the decisions? The answer: not many at the most but likely zero.

Now let's imagine what would happen if this job got hundreds of resumes but only one person called and kept calling and sending emails to stay top of mind? I'm not saying you would get the job but I'm telling you, you would likely be a leading candidate.

Sometimes you have to do the things you hate to get ahead or to succeed at life and career and that includes doing things that most people aren't willing to do. This will motivate you and make you feel super human. It goes back to being known as the go to person who everyone can count on. Become that person and watch the drive and get-up-and-go really start to climb.

Want to get shot out of a canon when you get out of bed tomorrow morning? Do something that you have been avoiding for a long time or go help someone who has been doing the same. By doing something that other people won't or can't do will be nothing less than motivating. Try it tomorrow.

33. COMPETITION IS NOT HEALTHY

They say competition is healthy. For who? Maybe the customer who is shopping around but not for the store owner that keeps chipping away at prices and his margin because that's what his competition down the street did yesterday. Ideally, a business owner doesn't want to compete because that's average. That's getting the blue participation award ribbon. The business wants to dominate their sector to be very successful and grow their business. They want to control their market. Do you think Apple competes or do they control or rule their space?

If you have your own business, then start ruling your space. If you work for a company, then master your department or area. If you are a student, then rule your classroom and your school. Don't let anyone get in your way and be the very best so that everyone behind you is eating your dust.

You have to be well ahead of everyone else in your particular space. School, work, business, hobbies, exercise or whatever else. You want to be your very best in you niche to be on top of your game. This will motivate you here and in other areas of your life.

Remember this short rhyme. When you compete you aren't complete. When you don't rule, you are a fool. Strive to be the best in everything and stop being a spectator in your own life.

How to Get Motivated and STAY Motivated

34. HELP SOMEONE EACH DAY

Each day look to help at least one person. Friend or stranger, it doesn't matter. Big or small help, is not the point. It could be something as small as a hello or asking someone if they're doing ok. Maybe you can give someone some encouragement or that preverbal pat on the back to help.

Smile at people as you walk down the street and see how many smile back at you. It takes less energy to smile than it does to frown anyways. You're trying to motivate yourself and you will accomplish that if you're helping others each day. Look to lend a hand at least once a day and watch how you will feel after you do. Say yes when someone asks a favor of you and say yes before you find out what that favor is.

Think of the last time someone helped you out, whatever it may have been, from opening a door for you to helping you on moving day. Think about how that made you feel. Have you ever had someone pay it forward to you? If you ever went to pay for something at a drive-thru and the cashier said the person in front (who has already driven away so you can't even thank them) of you have already paid for your coffee or meal. That's an incredible feeling and you want to do it for someone else as soon as possible.

Make that a goal for today and help one person out and pay it forward. These good deeds will make both of you feel terrific.

35. BUY PREMIUM FUEL

Eat only what is good for you. You don't need to buy a book on eating better. You know the garbage I'm talking about. What happens to your car when you spend a little more and switch to premium fuel? After one fill up does it run a little better? What about after 10 fill ups? Don't eat one healthy lunch a week and think you'll feel good because you won't. Eat good and you'll feel good. Eat great and you'll feel great.

Don't forget to take vitamins too. It's not just for times that you haven't eaten right or during cold and flu season but each day. It will help fill in the gaps and will complement your overall health.

I didn't say you have to completely get rid of that occasional indulgence in the drive-thru but the worse stuff you put in your body the worse you will feel. If you're trying to increase your drive and motivation in all aspects of your life then it starts with what is going inside your tank so you can drive further, faster and have more pep in your engine.

Don't go for broke and start doubling or tripling your grocery bill but you know what the good stuff is so start buying it. This is not a diet, it's doing what is right to feel right. If you have a big unhealthy fast food lunch your body will suck your energy away because it needs to digest all of that burger, fries and sugary soda you just ate. Then you'll suffer from the crash in the midday and it continues with the sugar in the coffee and the donut or chocolate bar in the afternoon for a little pick-me-up. You know the vicious cycle so stop now and then watch your energy and motivational levels rise.

36. EXERCISE EACH AND EVERYDAY

All these rules or chapters are exercises to build up or strengthen your motivation. So you also need to start (or continue) to exercise a little each day. This will build up your body and thus your self-esteem. When you build up your self-esteem you increase your motivation.

Anything that inspires or stimulates you, you want to do. Everything you have read above this or what you will read below are meant to do just that, inspire you. It's all part of the big picture and so is this. If you have never exercised before then start slow but make sure it's often. Start by parking further away to walk a little or take the stairs and skip the elevator today.

If you start by doing a small amount of exercise but frequently it will help you to do it more often and eventually longer but it will almost immediately raise your motivation. Today I want you to start for between 5-10 minutes but here's the key: do it twice! That way it's 10-20 minutes of exercise but by the third day you can say you have exercised six times that week. You will think you're exercising but you are really strengthening your motivational muscle.

If you have already read this far into the book, then you must be motivated. That's why I know you can do this one too. The hardest thing about exercising is starting. Take a short break from reading now and go move around and do something. Better yet, buy the audio book so you can do both!

This has nothing to do with diet or losing weight. It's all about making you feel good, giving you more energy but most of all making you feel good about motivation.

37. DON'T LOOK IN THE REVIEW MIRROR

You have heard this one all your life. The past is the past. Leave the review mirror for parking. Always look forward because there is nothing for you in the past. Plan today to live for tomorrow so you can have another yesterday. A yesterday you won't look behind at because it's not going to catch up so drive forward and press on that gas.

The faster you go the less crowded it tends to be so look to the future for endless possibilities. Your motivation, your goals and dreams are all in the future so you better get there. They're waiting for you there, but not forever.

Think of a chess master. Do you think they are only thinking of the current move or even worse three moves ago? Their minds are several moves ahead. While you are thinking about protecting your pawn the master already has you checkmated in his mind. In life, think like a chess master. Always look forward and into the future. You will be able to write better goals if you do this too.

When you write your goals don't word them in future tense but in present tense. As an example, don't write: I want to make $250,000 next year. You need to write: I made over $250,000 this year and I was able to donate the most I ever have to the children's hospital. Now that's a well written goal!

38. KEEP THE VERY BEST PEOPLE AROUND YOU

Your spouse, friends, co-workers, suppliers, customers or anyone else you that you invite into your life needs to be above average, they need to be great to bring out even more greatness in you.

You need higher quality people around you. I don't mean stick your nose up and think you're better than everyone else but look for those with the same goals, values and beliefs as you so you can be more focused on your goals and reach them faster. You don't need a Remora in your life. The Remora is the fish that sticks to sharks like the Great White. They feed off the scraps left over. You don't need a Remora feeding off your scraps or you.

It makes sense that you are trying to reach a new level of greatness in your life. That's why, to achieve that, you need to keep only great people around you. Greatness attracts great people and great people attract greatness.

Join Mastermind or other similar groups to meet likeminded people. As the saying goes; great minds think alike. Get out in the community and introduce yourself to people like yourself or above yourself for maximum impact on your life.

How to Get Motivated and STAY Motivated

39.   JOIN A POWER GROUP

It's similar to the previous one. Get in a group of winners or other like-minded individuals who are shooting for greatness like you. There are Mastermind groups that is for this very thing. If you are an entrepreneur, then perhaps join a BNI (Business Network International) group who are all trying to help each other with one common goal.

The people in these groups will feed your enthusiasm to do more and it will create a thirst to find more people like them. Once you have outgrown those people move on to find another group whose people inspire you more than the previous group of people. Don't drop the previous people out of your life, just expand your circle of influencers in your life.

If you can't find one of these groups in your community, then perhaps start one yourself. People are always looking to connect or network or even self-promote themselves and their businesses. You will be surprised, once you start just how many people are on a similar quest as you. It is important to remember that you are looking for people like yourself; ones that are highly motivated and driven to succeed and are interested in helping others do the same.

40.   GET OUT OF THERE

Get out of your comfort zone. Your comfort zone is your house, your office or anywhere else you feel 'safe' because there is a routine and familiarity. Get out of predictable situations to increase your confidence and it will eventually help with your feelings about new situations and meeting new people. Your motivation and determination will increase with each passing event.

Turn off the junk on television and go visit a friend's house, a church event, go help out at a senior's home, coach a child's team or volunteer in your community. The point is leave and get out of all the predicable trap. Get out and make new friends, meet new people and network yourself into new experiences.

How to Get Motivated and STAY Motivated

41.   GET MASSIVE ATTENTION

Being the center of attention or even just getting a lot of attention is not only good for one's ego but also for your motivation. It makes you feel good and will make you do more good things.

When you start doing so much and being that go to person we've talked about, people might resent you. That's attention and that's a good thing. It might be from jealous people because they think you're doing far too much in their eyes or people that just don't understand that you are different from most people. When you are motivated and start doing more than you use to and then more than most people do, you will start getting massive attention.

Now you might not be looking to promote your business, you might not even own a business and don't wish to be a politician but that doesn't matter. It's about getting out of that comfort zone and thus creating greater motivation. Go speak at your child's school or a community event. It will pump you up, I promise you.

42. DIFFICULTIES ARE A GOOD THING

Everyone tries to avoid problems. I'm telling you to seek them out. Now I'm not talking about getting into some mischief late at night. I mean seeking problems to solve. It comes back to helping others and being a go to person. All of that can help to motivate you to move to the next level.

Big problems can motivate you rather than the same old boring lame problems you have always had. Have you ever been talking to someone about something and said "that's a good problem to have"? Perhaps they have two job offers at two great companies and they just can't decide and they are almost mad at the situation. That is an example of having a good problem to have.

Think of some problems you could have and it would cause you to toss and turn in bed. Those are the problems that, once solved, would motivate you to look to solve even more.

The inability to cope with a problem or to just stick your head in the sand when one comes up is exactly the reason you need to solve more problems and look for more of them to solve. It's that knee jerk reaction to a problem that is one of the reasons your motivation gets sucked out of you. Seek problems and inspiration will find you.

43.   DON'T WAIT, DO IT NOW

I remember being in high school and studying for a test while I was getting dressed just before leaving to go write the test. I was reading the text book on the way to school! Now that's leaving it to the last second.

Don't wait to do it later if you can do it now. What will happen later? I don't know and neither do you so get it done, whatever it is, do it now instead of later. I use what I call the two-minute rule. If I can get something done as soon as it comes to my attention that it needs to get done, I do it immediately if it can be done within two minutes. If it will take longer I will get it done as soon as possible but I will always mark it in my calendar or planner. That way at the end of the day you don't have a bunch of little things lingering that still need doing.

If you are waiting to the last minute to complete a task that has a deadline, then chances are you rushed it and it might not be done correctly and you start being known as someone that has only "C" level work or worse, a "C" level work ethic. Get out of average.

Get it done so you can get more things done. Watch your motivation increase with each task you check off on your to-do-list.

44. ALWAYS GO ABOVE AND BEYOND

Do you remember when your parents or grandparents told you it is better to give than receive? They were right!

Most people will want to help you out once you help them out. Ever notice when you hold the door for someone when you walk in a shopping mall? They feel almost obligated to open the next one for you. You paid it forward and now they want to do the same for you. If you always go above and beyond what you normally do and go above and beyond what most people do watch how that changes you and makes you feel. Now, did you go above and beyond for you? For other people? Both? You did it for them but it just ended up making you feel special too and that's a good thing.

This is also true for almost everything you do. At work if the report is due at 3pm then hand it in a noon. If a swimmer is training for a five lap race in the pool do you think she only trains for a five lap race? Probably not. How about a runner for a 10k race? If he runs 15 or 20k then he'll have the stamina to run 10k.

Always push yourself to do more. Add another 1-2% or even 10% more. Just one more rep, lap or pound when you're working out. Just one more email, report or other task at work. This will help to increase your self-discipline to do a little more each and every time.

You aren't doing this for anyone other than yourself. When you know you did everything you could do and then picked it up an extra notch this will do nothing but inspire you.

45.   SMILE FROM A MILE

When I started dating my wife Daniela I would park down the street and walk the short distance to her house. My wife's sister would see me walking down the street and ask me when I arrived what was wrong or why I was mad. I was confused, I didn't realize I was frowning or at the very least not looking happy as I walked. I knew once I saw my girlfriend, her parents or siblings I would be smiling because I was happy to see them. However, it was the time before, when I thought nobody was around, I just didn't smile. Don't get me wrong, I'm a happy person but I wasn't letting the world know. It wasn't until someone pointed it out that I took notice.

I was just starting my field sales career at the time and I knew to always smile when dealing with customers but I thought if a customer saw me walking into their business with a frown, what message was I sending? It was then that I came up with smile from a mile. I was always a happy person but it never seemed to show on my face if I wasn't face-to-face with someone.

Now I always try my best to have a pleasant expression on my face. I'm not talking about have a constant big creepy smile like I'm the Joker from Batman but just enough that people can tell I'm happy, approachable and want to engage me in conversation.

Make a conscience effort to be aware of the picture you are

sending out to everyone that looks your way. Smile when someone looks at you and have a "pleasant face" when walking around just doing your thing. You'll be surprised at the number of people that smile back.

46.   PUT A SMILE IN YOUR VOICE

Smiling doesn't end on what other's see. People can also detect it when you are talking with them over the phone. My wife taught me this one. She worked years ago for a major international courier company where she was a phone agent. To prove her point, she had me say two identical sentences while I covered my face with a book. The first one with no expression on my face and the other while smiling. What an incredible difference. She could tell instantly that I sounded happy in the sentence that I was smiling. I encourage you to try it now and see what I mean.

You will put people at ease in new situations if they see you smiling. Imagine going to a crowded waiting room and seeing only two seats available. One is beside a person with a frown and the other looks up smiling. Who would you rather sit next to? The next time you're stand waiting for an elevator you don't know who will be on it when the doors open. When the elevator stops at your floor the person or people in the elevator don't know who is about to get on. Now think how nice it would be and how everyone breathes a sigh of relief when the doors part and everyone has a positive expression.

When you start doing this you will notice that you'll be in a better overall mood and thus increase your motivation. Smile more and smile often.

47.　Early to Bed

Staying up late doesn't usually accomplish very much. If you're staying up late chances are you are either up to no good or you aren't doing anything productive and that isn't good either. As the old saying goes: the early bird catches the worm.

Sure, there are always exceptions but if you want to be focused and get an early start that means going to bed early. It won't take long to adjust either.

Most people set their alarms for a set wake up time. You also need to set a time to go to bed and sleep. Don't go to bed and stay up an hour looking at a bright screen on an electronic device. Studies have said that affects the quality of sleep that you get. When you get to bed, go to sleep.

Don't kid yourself. It is very important to get a proper amount of sleep. If that's six hours for you or eight hours that's fine. Go to bed early so you can wake up well before the roosters. Shoot for a bedtime of 9 or 10 at the latest and get ahead start in the morning and a head start on everyone else and get an early start on your daily motivational routine.

48.   WORKSHOPS AND NETWORKING

This is not unlike anything else you learn from in terms of books, audio programs or classes. You go to workshops to learn and network and you go to a networking events to, of course; network! You are seeking like-minded individuals. However, you are also looking to reach up to people above you in either career, life or both.

If the area that you live in either doesn't have these kind of events or you've been to all of them, you could either start your own or take a vacation with your family and take a day or two and go to some workshops in that city. You will likely be able to write off (check with your accountant) part or all of the trip.

You will want to go to a workshop/seminar or a Mastermind type event about three or four times a year. The networking event if you are an entrepreneur or at least have that mindset can be done weekly or more often. When I went to weekly BNI (Business Network International) I would often get invited to other networking events such as a seminar or something from my local chamber of commerce.

One last wealth of information is Meetup where you can find likeminded individuals who are also looking for shared interest groups to join or start your own.

49.　LOOK AT YOUR MONEY

Every week or two make a point (make sure to put it in your planner) to look over your investments, bills, automatic payments, bank accounts and anything else you have money in or that you owe. If you're single, I still want you to go over this but if you have a spouse meet with them. If you have kids get them involved to learn this behavior at a young age.

The expression out of sight, out of mind is very true for your finances. Keep a close eye on it and it will treat you right. Chances are your accountant and financial adviser or financial planner only meets with you once or twice a year to look at and discuss your money so you need to do it up to 50 times more than they are. After all, it's your money, not theirs.

The more you look at your money the more goals you can set about your money and achieve your money making or money saving strategies. Take a moment now and schedule your first meeting. Write it in your planner. The more you plan the easier it will be to execute.

50. MONEY CAN'T BUY HAPPINESS

Look at the goals you have. If your goals say that you want more money, then what do you want the money for? If it's for a bigger house, then why do you want a bigger house? If you answered you wanted a better house in a different neighborhood for your kids because it would be safer, had better school and future opportunities for them, then that's the better answer. You must tie your goals to something bigger and better in order for them be more achievable.

How about your goal is to get a promotion and a raise at work? Then put something like you want to be better situated to save for your family's future or you want to donate more to charity. As for the promotion part perhaps you may want to be able to mentor new employees like you were mentored once when you started there and it will give you a tremendous amount of satisfaction knowing you are helping someone else.

Now don't just think this stuff, because it won't work. You must truly believe it. It is important to feel that deep in your heart that you have your goal tied to a huge non-monetary goal. If you don't believe it – it won't happen. Once you believe you are doing it for the greater good or someone else then it will come easier and faster than before.

It doesn't matter what your goal is. You must tie it in with something that is a higher purpose. Every goal can be tied to this; you just have to start tying it all together. Try this, in your planner on today's long term goals, I want you to write your goal with a tie-in. Let's suppose you wrote: 'I want to be a successful business owner in three years.' That's a good goal. Now let's make it great. Try and change the wording to the present and don't forget to tie-in something of importance. For example: 'I own a successful business and I now have flexible time to spend with my family and my children's future education is taken care of. I'm feel great knowing I employ people and I love being a successful entrepreneur.' Now that's a great goal!

51. GOALS AND OBJECTIVES

Don't keep all these goals or targets all to yourself. You need to meet with your family or close friends once a month to discuss each other's goals to see if there is either some common ground where you could help each other reach each other's goals. Perhaps there might even be a scenario where your goals are very similar and if you work on one of your goals with the help of one or two other people then once achieved then you can help the other person achieve their goals. You will both being reaching the goal even faster.

It's great to go to a goal setting workshop and meet other big thinkers wanting to do the same. However, I strongly believe you also need to get people close to you and who love and support you to get involved. Both are great at keeping you super motivated.

At your job everyone works together as part of a team and you all have a common goal that you're trying to reach. You can do this for your own goals and objectives. It's important that whoever you are having this meeting with to achieve your goals with that you do not judge anyone else's' goals. No matter how big or impossible it might sound. Don't say anything other than "Sounds fantastic, how can I help?" They could be thinking the very same thing about your goals. Don't hurt them, help them and in return, you'll help yourself.

52.   REWARD YOURSELF

Have rewards for accomplishments that compliment your potential. That means don't reward yourself for status quo or average work or average results because that's average thinking. However, do reward yourself in a big way when you reach your seemly out of reach potential.

You are setting yourself some lofty goals that will ultimately create an enormous amount of motivation for you. Don't short change yourself by setting subpar goals and then rewarding yourself for hitting them. Also, don't set high goals and reward yourself for trying. There is no participation award here either.

Sometimes the doing is the reward. Have you ever had a bunch of housework or spring cleaning in the yard and you wrote a to-do-list? After each task was done you crossed it off your list until you were all finished. How did crossing it off your list make you feel? It felt good didn't it? It was your own little reward for a completed task. Just the act of drawing that line through the task was reward enough. Remember, small rewards for small accomplishments. The bigger the accomplishment the bigger the reward. Zero reward for zero accomplishment.

53.   DECIDE NOT TO BE BORED

If you have ever been around children for an extended period of time you have likely heard them say they are bored. With an entire room full of toys, a backyard with a pool, a garage with a bike, a bunch of sports equipment and a shelf full of books they are still bored.

You decide that you are bored then don't announce it or complain about it because there are so many things to do. Boredom to motivation is life without breathing and a heart with no blood. You can't have one without the other.

The unmotivated, unwilling and uninspired are bored. Take the time to understand when you are bored and start looking for things to stimulate mind and body then you increase your creativeness.

Look to expand your options and help someone or start to write a book or brainstorm a new business. Look to be more creative in these situations when your mind is clear and come up with the next big thing in your life to inspire you.

Have you ever been in the shower and had some great idea or thought of something you haven't thought of before in years? It's because your mind was clear as it went through a task you have

How to Get Motivated and STAY Motivated

done every day for decades. That's why you need to recognize these feeling of boredom as opportunities for inspired thought.

You have two choices: be bored or don't be bored. The choice should be clear.

54.   DRINK MORE WATER

You know the soda and the stuff that tries to pass as fruit juice is delicious but you also know just how bad it is for you and your motivation. It makes your energy go up and down and it's full of empty calories. All that and I'm not even suggesting you cut it completely out of your diet! However, it should be reduced by a minimum of 80-90%.

We talked about rewarding yourself when it counts so if you have a soda on a hot summer day that's fine as long as it is tied to a goal. What you need to do is drink a lot more water. When you get thirsty you are already dehydrated so drink more and more often.

Water loosens your entire body. Drink a glass 15 minutes before a meal and it is said you consume about 15% less calories. Leave a bottle or glass of water at your bedside. As soon as you wake up drink the water. You will be surprised just how better you feel after a few days of doing that. It's wonderful for your metabolism.

Drink more water and you will gain more energy, likely lose some weight, decrease the bad toxins in your body and increase your motivation. If you can't control what is going in your body, then how will you control (or increase) your motivation?

How to Get Motivated and STAY Motivated

55. YOUR CALENDAR NEEDS TO BE FILLED

Keeping a full calendar will keep you motivated. Have you ever had a lazy Saturday where you weren't doing very much other than just hanging out watching television? Then someone calls in the late afternoon and wants to go out. You found it hard to get off the couch let alone get ready to go out, even if the going out part was supposed to be fun. Why did that happen? Because your body got accustomed to doing nothing. You had zero motivation. This can happen not just for a day but for a week, a couple of months and many years at a time if you get stuck in a boring routine that doesn't keep you busy and physically and mentally stimulated or challenged.

If you run out of stuff to put on your calendar, then go back to what we talked about when I said to help people or to volunteer somewhere. Be creative if you have to when filling it out. If you have an empty block, then make something up to do that makes you and everyone involved happy. Keep a full calendar and a fuller life.

Even on those lazy Saturdays we all enjoy occasionally it is important to still write in your planner to keep the routine. It will also be fun to enter things such as: build pillow fort with son, reading, watch bowling on television, update Facebook profile, watch cat videos online, fly kite, puzzle, goal writing, light run, fetch with dog and play dolls with daughter.

56.   PICTURE WHAT YOU WANT

In the movie The Secret someone talked about having a vision board. A vision board is a number of pictures of items or goals that you want in the near or distant future. You put these pictures on a board or somewhere else that you will see it every single day.

Don't take pictures of things that you just got or you had years ago, leave that for Facebook. Keep pictures of things that you do want and keep looking at them and believe that they are already yours. This will increase your motivation to keep striving to remove pictures because you already attained that item or hit that goal. After you take it down, it's time to put up a new picture and set a higher goal.

Put these pictures on a wall, in your computer, your phone, your planner, wallet or a book of goals. Keep them close so you can look at, the very minimum, at least once a day. That's why, in my Motivated Planner that I've developed (more info at the end of the book) I've left plenty of space for you to stick a picture of something that is your goal.

When you envision an item or goal so vividly over and over you will attain it. It's not a matter of if but when you will reach it. Raise your goals and expectations and your attainment of those things will also rise.

57.   KEEP TRACK OF EVERYTHING THAT IS IMPORTANT

If you want to get motivated and stay motivated, then as mentioned make sure you have a full calendar. After you start doing it, keep track of how often you are doing the things that you do. It doesn't end there either. Keep track of everything such as what percentage of your money goes to rent or mortgage, how much time do you spend in a week sleeping or watching television? Do you know how much money you spend at the gas station on items that aren't gas? Once you know all this information you can start making adjustments in your spending, your time and anything else. Keep track of everything of value to you so you can make logical decisions and not emotional ones. Once you realize where your money or time is going, you will need to make changes to align your goals and what's important to you in your life.

If you don't keep track and measure all these statistics in your life you aren't in control because you never knew you watched 14 hours a week of mindless television. If you just stopped watching 30 minutes a day, what would happen? How would your life change? If you got back 30 minutes a day what would you do with it? That's 900 minutes (15 hours) per month! That's 182.5 hours a year!

There is 168 hours in a week so you gained over a week of time just by not watching 30 minutes of television each day. What are you going to do with an extra week every year? Where else can you find more time? If you don't keep track, you'll never know.

It is usually the people that watch the most television or spend the most time on social media that complain there isn't enough time. No time to exercise or take up a hobby yet they spend 25 or more hours per week in front of a screen that has nothing to do with their job.

58.   BE IRREPLACEABLE

Let everyone you meet, work with or those you spend time with, know that you are irreplaceable by your actions and not just your words.

Be so dependable and reliable that your boss wants to clone you because you are so irreplaceable. Be so loving and loyal that your spouse loves you more each day because you are irreplaceable. Be so helpful that your community thinks you are so reliable and trustworthy and knows that you are so irreplaceable.

In this day and age of replaceable shaving blades, batteries and many more things that get thrown away and/or replaced, be different and be irreplaceable to everyone.

It is your character and your actions that leave a lasting impression and make you more memorable in the eyes of the people you meet every day. These actions and your character is the foundation that being totally irreplaceable is built on. Your motivation can't be replaced if you feel irreplaceable.

59. LISTEN TO PROGRAMS THAT MOTIVATE YOU

I will be making the audio version of this book within a few weeks of releasing this book. Chances are it's available now and if it isn't you can click and follow the link at the end of the book to be notified of when it's available. As I have said it's recommended that you get the print, ebook, audio and video program of many motivational or self-help publications. I'm not just saying that about mine but you need to stay pumped up from a variety of media and from various people to keep you both motivated and fascinated.

There have been many different people I've been interested in over the years that I'll buy motivational books or other programs that have interested me and I make sure I get all the medias they are available in it keep me learning no matter where I am.

I once heard a story about a New York City police officer who commuted over two hours each day on public transit. That's 14 hours per week that he put to good use. Rather than watch movies or listen to music he took online courses and eventually got an additional degree to help him get a promotion at work. Now there is someone who was motivated and used his time wisely.

If you are commuting, at the gym, waiting in a doctor's office or

How to Get Motivated and STAY Motivated

have some free time I recommend listing to these types of programs to better yourself and give yourself a boost. Music is fine to pump you up or relax you for short periods. All my listening is about 15-25% music and/or talk radio with a little bit of traffic and weather mixed in and the rest, about 50-75%, are programs that I can learn something from and educate myself like an audio book.

60. LISTEN TO MUSIC THAT MOTIVATES YOU

The last small portion of your commute or the amount of time you are listening to something I switch to something that will pump me up. Just crank it and use your steering wheel as a drum and give it your all. You've just listened to 30 minutes of some motivational program and then one or two head banging, fist pumping songs and you will be ready for anything! Now don't just walk, run to the next thing after that.

Pick your music wisely to complement your mood. If you are going to a job interview or have a work presentation to do then I suggest not getting some lullaby song but instead get something that lifts you up and compels you to start tapping your foot.

61.   EVERYTHING IS POSSIBLE

Examine everything like it is totally 100% possible. It goes back to being positive and a can do type person who has a can do type personality. Get out of the habit that you have likely had all your life when you are faced with an impossible or improbable task. Change what you say from here on. Change a statement like "That's impossible, it can't be done" to a questions like "This is very challenging; how can it be done?" or "That's different, how can I help?"

This simple question (and not a statement) will pump up your motivation because it gets you thinking and asking more questions. How can it be done? Well, perhaps if we did this or how about I try that? This might sound crazy but what if we tried this instead of the way it was always done? Are you (the reader) getting it now? Try one or two questions yourself now.

Making a statement you cut off any possibly positive change. Ask questions and you open up to endless possibilities and shut out negativity. Anything is possible.

62. IF IT CAN'T BE DONE, THEN DO IT

When someone says something can't be done look to prove them wrong. Not to prove them wrong to make them feel bad or less of themselves but to motivate and inspire you. Look for these kind of challenges because once you complete one of them then watch what will happen to you and your motivation. You will be looking for the next "impossible" thing to do.

As a child you heard the word "no" up to 700,000 times before the age of just five years old! That's 400 times per day! That's a lot of negative "it can't be done" feelings that you must break through.

Take a moment now to write down what others have recently said to you that is impossible or what you have given up before you have even tried. Now put it on your to-do-list and watch what happens to not only you but to others around you, once you complete the task.

63. TIME MANAGEMENT IS FOR ROOKIES

Time management has become a catchphrase, something you put on your resume or said about yourself during a job interview. Stop managing time and start to control it. Use your calendar on your phone, tablet or what I prefer is the old fashion paper one. Sure set your reminders on your phone because paper can't beep at you but use pen and paper to plan out your minutes, hours, days, your life and life's goals. If you write something out I believe you will retain it more than typing it out. It will connect you to whatever you wrote more. At the end of the book you'll hear about my new calendar (planner) that I'm launching as a result of this book.

Driving down the road do you want to manage your car or do you want to control it? Do you want to manage a business or control one? Are you managing your diet/weight or do you want to control it? Are you starting to understand?

You have a block of time, say 15 minutes. Do you want to manage it or control it? Make every second of those 15 minutes work for you and get everything out of them so you can move on to the next 900 seconds (15 minutes) to get more done. This will free you up, keep you on track for your various tasks and motivate you because you now control time, not the other way around.

64. CONTACT PEOPLE WHO CAN CHANGE YOUR LIFE

Make a list of people that can change your life. Most of these people you don't even know them and they don't know you but don't worry about that for now.

Perhaps it's a big client, an exercise guru, a top investor, a master at whatever niche hobby or other interest you have or whoever can bring you to the next level of knowledge and understanding in your life. Think of all these people. Maybe you don't even know their names and you need to do some research. Follow the link at the end of the book to see how you can hear me speak at an event or speak with me directly to pump you up!

Make the list of people who can change your life and I promise you, you'll be so motivated that if you do it just before bed you might not fall asleep fast or at all. It is that powerful.

Now once you have the list email them, call them, write a letter, send a card or visit their office. If they are number one in their field, then chances are they were like you once. Remember, every pro was an amateur once. If you don't ask you will never know if they will offer anything. Even a 10-minute phone call might be enough from them to light your path. Don't forget to value their time and be respectful at all times.

See if you can schedule one 15-minute phone call once a month. Do this with another three or four people and you have a total of one hour a month of inspiration and mentorship from the people that you look up to. Now that's motivating!

65.   INVEST IN YOUR LIFE, OFTEN

Want some ROI (Return on Investment) that you can count on? Invest in yourself, not once but at regular intervals.

What do I mean by investing in yourself? Read more, listen more and learn more. Audio books, print books, Ebooks, conferences, seminars, videos and programs are all there to help you. So invest in yourself to increase your overall output and more specifically your motivation.

Invest in yourself as often as you can and watch your stock rise.

66. MAKE TIME FOR YOUR FAMILY

Make quality (not quantity) time for your family. Absolutely put it in your calendar. If you are thinking "Kevin, I'm not putting a reminder to play with my kids or have some alone time with my spouse in a calendar." Then I must ask; how committed are you then? Will you do what it takes? By you putting it in your calendar you have made a commitment to yourself and a promise to your family.

Ten minutes of talking with your kids or spouse is way more meaningful than watching a 30-minute show in the same room as them. Remember to make the time quality time.

Don't do it three times a week. It has to be done daily. That's why I said quality at the beginning. Quality time isn't watching television every day. It might be every week or a movie every month. It's interaction it's talking about life or playing a board game or laying on the floor and play cars or dolls. When was the last time you played hide and seek or played tag?

How about the family that doesn't live with you? Don't forget to put in your calendar to call your Mom, visit your brother or invite your Uncle over. Try sending flowers for no reason to a family member. It's important to do these things because it will motivate all involved.

67.   INTRODUCE YOURSELF TO EVERYONE

Get everyone to know of you, know about you and to know you. Become extroverted to the 10th power. Talk to everyone. Don't give up an opportunity to speak to someone new.

If you have a small business and think you need everybody in your local community or your city to know you then you're wrong. You need plant Earth and beyond to know you. This will make you want to build more contacts, business partners and friends.

It doesn't matter if you are in business or not. The point is you can't have too many contacts or friends for that matter.

Get out of the normal way you have been doing things and start introducing yourself to people on the elevator or at the gym. Build up the courage and do it once and you will want to keep doing it because it feels that good. Don't be discouraged if someone doesn't respond or is unfriendly. Move on and make contact with someone else. It might be just what that person needed.

68. Don't Watch News, Make It

If you put in too much effort and got massive attention because of your help in the community or created too much buzz for your business, product or service then perhaps someone needs to interview you or write an article about you. Perhaps you can start a blog or vlog or be interviewed by someone who has a blog. It is all news of some kind. Start small and soon you might be on national news or some video you're in goes viral. Too many times you watch negative news pieces and it sucks the motivation and energy out of you. I'm suggesting you don't watch the news – I'm suggesting you MAKE the news.

Be different and be something positive on the news to motivate and inspire others. Become that role model that future generations can look up to.

69.   QUICK! HAVE A SENSE OF URGENCY

Don't walk, run! Have a sense of urgency on everything you do. Move from task to task in your day urgently like everything was being timed and you're trying to beat the time from your last task. This moving quickly will increase your motivation. Now I'm not talking about rushing work and having a lot of mistakes and causing problems for yourself at your job. I mean speed up a little. You know the various things in your day that can be sped up without sacrificing safety or accuracy.

We all have been waited on in a store or restaurant and the person serving you is so slow that they are almost in reverse. Now imagine how important you would feel if that person stepped up their game and moved with a sense of urgency.

70.   DON'T BE SATISFIED WITH SATISFACTION

You want to shoot for greatness. When you have done your best you have a great sense of accomplishment and motivation. So why are you satisfied with satisfaction?

Satisfaction should be the name of a minimum security prison because that's exactly what it is. It is holding you back with just enough safety, security and feeling of hominess that it has tricked you into feeling okay or even feeling happy with satisfaction.

Shoot for greatness and excellence beyond your wildest dreams. Would you go on a blind date with someone if your friend said "I think you should meet this person. Looks wise they are a 5/10 and they have an average personality. I think you will be satisfied with them." Would you want to meet them? I doubt it. Shoot for greatness in everything in your life.

Think about a high priced product that has average reviews and rates two and a half stars out of five. Would you buy it? Probably not. You probably don't want satisfaction from anything or anyone, so don't settle for it from yourself. Strive for excellence. Each time. Every time.

71.   DON'T EVER LOWER YOUR GOALS AND TARGETS

If you are in sales, then you've likely been in a meeting half way in the month and management lowers the target due to low sales. They want to keep everyone in the game and excited as they get closer to the new lower number. This has the opposite effect and should never be done.

If you are falling short on any of your targets, not just those in sales, you need to increase your efforts and not decrease your targets. Here are two examples; if you want to lose weight and you would be happy with 10 pounds (4.5kg) but thrilled if it was 25lbs (11.3kg), but you only set a target of 10. Then you only hit eight pounds, you might be disappointed. However, now imagine if you set your target at 25 pounds and you still came up a bit short at 21 pounds (9.5kg). Would you still be disappointed or would you wonder what else you need to raise the target on?

Never lower your goals or targets because it will lower your motivation at the same time. I suggest you review all of your goals both personal and professional and increase them. Get motivated and stay motivated, raise your goals and your efforts.

72. DON'T COMPARE YOURSELF TO ANY MONETARY ITEM

Never compare yourself to money or something that costs money. Never say things like "I can't afford these shoes." or "I can't live in that neighborhood." or "I'll never make $100,000 in a year." You are worth more than that. You are worth more than some money or materialistic things.

Now I'm not suggesting you want for nothing and throw common sense out and rack up your credit cards on a shopping spree. You set those shoes or the house in that area of town as a goal. Change what you say and think to something like "I won't buy those shoes yet." or "That is my house in two years." Or better yet, "That is my house!" That will get you to visualize your goal, that's more powerful. Change the words and your feelings and then motivation will also change.

73. SHOOT FOR GREATNESS

Shoot for greatness each and every day. You might have a good day today but you should always aim for having a great day. If your goal is to have a good day or be good at your golf game or perhaps you want a good day at work, you might not even reach it. If, however you strive to have a great day you might only hit good but that's better than just okay or worse.

Be the greatest at everything you do. That should be your goal in what you do. Greatness is a feeling and a doing. Do great things and feel great. Feel great and do great things.

It often takes the same about of energy or effort between good and great. Sometimes the difference between good and great is the quality of work rather than the quantity of work. Do you want a good paycheck or a great paycheck? Would you rather have a good marriage or a great marriage? Are you a good friend or are you a great friend? Are you getting it now?

74.   OVERCOMMIT TO EVERYONE AND EVERYTHING

Overcommit to everyone and everything you do. This includes your family, friends, work and community. This means not just to overcommit but you must follow it up by over delivering. You're just scamming them or tricking them if you're deliberately overcommitting with zero follow through.

As an example let's say you have a task to do and your boss asks you how long something will take. You know it will take you 20 minutes but you tell her it will take 45 minutes and then you look like the hero when you deliver it in just 30 minutes. That is cheating. That scenario doesn't benefit anyone and wouldn't motivate you to do more or feel better.

That same example should go like this; task given and you say it should take no more than 20 minutes. You push and stay focused and you deliver it in 16 or 18 minutes. Now you feel great and your boss feels great and you did something great for your company and you are on your way to having a great day.

If you feel like you aren't motivated it might be because you have been under committing to yourself and others. Start making promises that are big and that you do keep. If you overcommit

AND over delivery, I promise you, you'll start delivering at levels you never imagined were possible.

75.   PICTURE THE ENDING

We all know how to do this. We've pictured the ending of a movie 15 minutes in or watched our favorite team and pictured the ending in the 4th inning. It is more of a hope or expectation that often doesn't come true.

I'm suggesting that you picture something so vividly that you think it has already happened. Look at the end of your goal or target and picture the ending. Once you picture the outcome now start thinking what it will take to get to the ending and seeing what you pictured actually happen. You must envision the end. Use a vision board if you have to. A vision board is a collage of pictures of your goal. Pictured getting that job? Put the logo of that company or a picture of the building the company is in on your vision board, on your phone or in your planner.

Now picture yourself 100% committed and motivated to help you get there. Take a picture of yourself with your hands raised cheering and excited. Put that picture on your phone, computer or vision board to strive to feel that feeling all the time.

76.   DO MORE, THEN A BIT MORE

Get a trainer, motivator, helper or someone that is also looking for motivation and you can help each other. This person can assist in pushing you to the finish line of tasks that would be a huge accomplishment when you do them. If you train yourself to do just a little more than what is required each time then you will succeed. If you train for a 5k race and only train for a 5k race you might be disappointed. If you train for 6, 7 or 8k runs then a 5k race will seem much easier.

Get in the habit of doing more so you can do more. The moment you realize you can run an extra quarter mile more or lift an extra 5lbs or do a project a little faster than the last time, that will be the break through and elevate your motivation to the next level.

Keep pushing yourself in every situation to do more and it will be a domino effect on how good you feel.

77.   LOOK UP TO GET MORE FRIENDS

Look for friends that are more successful than you. I know it seems petty but you need to better yourself and learn from the pros in life. Don't go ditch your old group of friends, that is as long as they aren't always negative and talk bad about you or others. Those you don't need in your life so it's just as well that you get new friends. Now I'm talking about people that are extremely successful in motivation, confidence, their job/career, family, where they live or their health and fitness level.

Get more friends in your circle. This will motivate you to meet new people, share each other's experiences, network and learn from them on how they got where to they are today. Set a goal for this month that you will make at least one new friend. Look for this person at a Mastermind group or a network meeting or go to special event or take a class.

78.   READ MANY MORE BOOKS

Did you know the average person reads one book a year? Do you know how many books above average people read? Those people are owners of companies, Vice Presidents, the CEO, CFO or other very successful people. The successful ones read about 60, that's right; six-zero, books a year!

Everyone is concerned that a particular Ebook is $10, that hardcover book is $40 or even an audio book might be a few dollars. You should be more focused on what million-dollar idea it will spark. Perhaps it might save you thousands on your heating bills in your life or help you close a sale that will put $10,000 in commission in your pocket next week. They say everyone has a million-dollar idea once in their life if they just acted on it. Now imagine how many more ideas would come from all those books that you have read.

You can still read a few novels or autobiographies if that's your thing but I suggest that you read much more non-fiction so you can learn and grow more. If you read more books every year, then watch your creativity soar. Get more creative and you will be motivated to do more and that includes reading.

79. ALWAYS SAY THANK YOU AND YES PLEASE!

Be more grateful. Let people know that you care. When I was a young boy I'd get a gift from my Aunt and Uncle for my birthday. My Mom would always ask me to write a thank you card. It was the right thing to do. I was always grateful for the gift but I didn't feel like writing the card but when I did boy did I feel good about doing it.

It doesn't matter how small of a thing someone did for you it must be met with an even greater thank you. If you didn't send thank you cards, texts or emails then you aren't in communication. The person you didn't thank might feel bad or perhaps even think twice about doing it again for you or someone else.

Too many people are too quick to say no, maybe or let me think about it. Start saying yes more often. Say yes to almost everything. Do you want to be more motivated and be able to do more? Then say yes to more things and get involved, help more and be busy more.

Don't be silly and say yes to actions that are illegal or immoral. Instead say yes to life! Say yes to new experiences or things that you always said no to in the past. Did you ever say no to a certain food when you were a kid? Then years later you have it again and loved it. Keep saying yes and your drive and motivation will hear you.

80.   THE 20 SECOND VACATION

Sometimes that's all you need. I have found it useful up to twice a day to lay down (sitting in a chair is acceptable but not preferred) and take my 'vacation'. Now I have never practiced meditation but I imagine it is similar.

I lie down on a couch, floor or bed and I don't move for at least 20 seconds but no longer than 60 seconds, I close my eyes and either think of a beach, somewhere else or simply nothing at all. It's amazing how more focused and refreshed you are after you do it.

81. YOUR 15-MINUTE (BLOCKED) DAY

Schedule your day, using your planner, in 15 minute blocks. Too many people write a few things down that are too vague. They think they have filled their day.

Start with four 15 minute blocks each hour. After you have mastered that you might want to try six 10 minute blocks every hour and finally 10 six minute blocks. It would depend on what you are doing but the point is you will do more.

It isn't about time management. Time management is for rookies and wannabes. You want to control time or be a time controller. When you give yourself that label, watch how efficient you become in controlling your entire day. This isn't limited to the work day but the entire day like family time, hobby time, reading time and so on.

Have you ever seen someone pack or unpack their suitcase and you wonder just how they were able to fit so much in their case? They folded things in a certain way and placed them in certain spots so there was no wasted space and every item they wanted to bring was in there. Now imagine that suitcase is your day. There will be no wasted space, everything you wanted to do that day got done and although it might be heavy it has a good handle and wheels so you can easily control it.

82. BE EXTRAORDINARY IN YOUR LIFE

It is YOUR life so you should be the master at it. You are the professional when it comes to your own life. Do you want to have an ordinary life or extraordinary life? It truly is 100% up to you. As they say, life is what you make it.

Look at every nook and cranny of your life and make it exceptional in every way. Have an extraordinary health, marriage, job/career, relationships and home life. Do you want an ordinary marriage or extraordinary marriage?

Ordinary people accept life as average and are happy with being satisfied and therefore just live. Extraordinary people want it all and usually get it. Be a glutton on the food we call life. Seek extraordinary in your life and watch how motivated you become.

83.   TEN MINUTES EARLY IS TOO LATE

If you have an appointment, dinner reservations or going to your friend's house, don't be late. My motto has always been if I'm 10 minutes early, I'm late. If my shift at work is at 7am and walk in at 6:56am I'm technically not late. However, I have to go punch in, take my lunch to the lunch room, take my jacket off, perhaps put a name badge on or even some kind of uniform and likely say hello to a few people it will be 7:05am or later before I even do any work.

Show up early for everything. Soon people will depend on you and even set their watches by your punctuality. The later one I jest but you'll find people using you as the gold standard. I had a retailer once tell me in an interview they were conducting earlier that day when they had an issue with a candidate regarding being on time. The retailer noticed on the candidate's resume that they live just one street over from the store. The candidate's reply was "Yeah, that's why I'm applying. I figured you were close enough to my house that I won't usually be late for my shift." This is someone who isn't controlling or even managing time.

When you arrive even a minute late you start searching for excuses about traffic, a power failure, a sick child, a runaway dog or something else. Don't be tempted to lie. The point is you were late and you should have left early enough to take into account for a couple of hiccups along the way.

How to Get Motivated and STAY Motivated

Arrive early and be ready. This is yet another thing that tells people that you are a stand up person, a go to person who is dependable and reliable. Be late and you tell the world around you that you just don't care.

84.   GET A FRONT ROW SEAT

Motivate yourself to do whatever you can or whatever it takes to be the first. That means sit up front at the class or seminar you're taking. Sit in first class, sit front row at the concert or sporting event. Don't go broke doing this but this should be a motivator to succeed at life and go for it and go for it all the way by creating the life you have always wanted and dreamed of.

Once you start sitting in the very best seats it will motivate you to do it more often. How can you do it more often? More importantly, how can you afford to do it more often? If you truly want it that bad you will figure out a way and motivate yourself to do it. The person that looks back at you in the bathroom mirror is counting on you to do it.

85. STAY CLOSE TO CHAMPIONS

I've mentioned this more than once. Go look for the people that are champions of health, of their industry, city or other type of leader. You want to be around winners and the type of people that have really successful lives.

These people are in a league of their own. They are the one percenters who everything they touch turns to gold. Watch these people and learn from them. Remember, their time is precious. If you can't get near them then research them, read up on them and learn. If they have written a book, get it. If they have mentioned their own mentor in their book or an interview, then get it. The point is be a sponge for inspiration and soak everything in.

86.   DAILY GOALS AND TARGETS

In business you might have annual or monthly targets to hit. I mentioned at the beginning of the book to write your goals and targets at least once a day but preferably twice a day. Don't write just one either, write a few. You must stay fixated on your daily target so you can achieve them. It's important to you or else you wouldn't have written it down in the first place.

Remember, goals and targets can be the same and they can be different. It your goal is to lose 20lbs before summer, your target might be 5lbs the first week and 5lbs for the last month.

Why do you wanted to be so fixated on your daily goals? It's food for your motivation. As you see that you're accomplishing more each day it will gain momentum. What would make today a great (not just good) day? Concentrate and come up with goals for today or tomorrow that if done will just pump you up so much because you had been putting these tasks off for another day.

Use your Motivated Planner to write your goals down once or twice per day. Concentrate on each one before you write it and envision the goal like you have already achieved it as you write it down.

87.　GET HUNGRY AND STAY HUNGRY

Let everyone you meet know that you are hungry. You are hungry to be motivated more each day. You have an incredible thirst for knowledge and wisdom. Don't suppress it because that is very negative for your motivation.

You learned in school to keep it down, your Mom likely told you in a grocery store to settle down so you might not be used to people's reaction and even comply. Don't! Do not conform and curb your enthusiasm as it will suck all motivation out of a given room.

Stay hungry about the success you have not yet achieved but will achieve. When you do this you will burst at the seams with so much drive and motivation. Nothing can stop the person who is motivated to do the thing that inspires them.

88.   GO WHERE THE MONEY IS, THEN NETWORK

Let suppose you go to a seminar or conference that is out of town or you take a family vacation. Stay in the nicest hotel. Why? It has to do with what we've discussed earlier. Get around successful people and network. Start building up your contacts and friends list. This is also a good idea to find a mentor there too.

These places are where the champions are. Don't spend a lot of time in your room, get in the lobby or where the action is. Get connected to winners who will inspire your next great thing or idea you have.

89. COMMUNITY INVOLVEMENT

Get out of your house and get into your community. Get involved by volunteering at a community center, your church, senior center, library, charity, political party or food bank. Become a mentor for a young person or read to kids at an after school program.

This will not only make you feel great and thus boost your motivation but it might also be a great opportunity to meet new friends, mentor someone, network for your company (employer) or your own business. Pretend you are in politics and you are always looking for that rope line. Get out and be engaging. Look to help others.

90. DON'T WALK, RUN!

Your calendar needs to be so full that you need to run, not walk, to everything you do. I use to work for a company as a sales rep. We had a big trade show once a year that the 'big boss' would attend. What he would do to reps standing around not doing anything was legendary. I always remember some great advice from a senior sales rep; it's harder to hit a moving target than one that is stationary. So if our client was late or a no show you had to move around fast like you were going somewhere and never empty handed. It's the old adage of fake it till you make it.

ABM=Always Be Moving. If you can't fill a calendar in the beginning, then move around quickly and write in filler in your calendar, things like helping other people on their daily goals or calendar tasks. Soon, especially after seeing other people's to-do list, you will have yourself pointed in the right direction.

Run to the next thing. Use the momentum you gained from accomplishing the last task to get you to the next one. Just remember this rhyme; "Too much calendar white space, then boredom you will face." Boredom will be followed by lack of inspiration and motivation. Keep your calendar full.

91. ALWAYS MEET NEW PEOPLE

Do you think you are the only one in a crowded room full of people you don't know that is uncertain and uncomfortable with meeting new people? Of course not! Most people are but trust me, the fear of the unknown is greatly outweighed by the payoff of meeting someone new. So go do it!

Go up to that stranger and say "Hi, my name is _____, what's your name?" The worst thing that will happen is you'll both forget each other's name in seconds. That's normal, especially in the beginning. If you forget it, don't sweat it. After they are done talking say something like "I'm sorry, I was listening and so interested in your _____ (story, job or whatever they were talking about) that I forgot your name. What is it again? Make sure you repeat their name at least two or three times in the conversation to remember it later. You could also exchange contact information or ask for their business card.

If you are going to a party, networking event, convention or other social gathering then don't worry that you are uncomfortable being there because chances are so is everyone else. You are all there to do the same thing and you are there to meet new people so stay in your uncomfortable zone. It will get easier the more you do it, I promise.

You will be more motivated the more extraverted you become. You will feel better about yourself even after just one of these situations because you'll likely meet 10, 20 or more new people at each one of these situations.

92.   BUSINESS CARDS

If you have a job that requires you to have a business card, you still might want to get a different one for social situations. If your job doesn't require you to have one or you are retired or out of work, you might consider still getting one.

Giving someone a card at a social setting can be more powerful than exchanging contact info that gets swallowed up in a sea of contacts on the other person's mobile device. I would do both because it's gives the other person double the chances of remembering you.

It doesn't have to be anything too fancy. Simple is best. Your name, number, email, one or two social media links (or your personal website that has those links), a title and perhaps a motto or quote and that's it. The title I would put something unrelated to your job if it's a social setting like 'future millionaire' or 'future author' – something that might spark conversation. The same with having a moto or a quote that you like.

93.   ELEVATOR PITCH

If you are trying to build your confidence and motivation but still want to grow your network, you still need an elevator pitch. We have almost all heard of this terminology as it pertains to sales people. If you find yourself in the elevator with a decision maker you might only have 20 seconds before they get off on their floor to impress them.

Usually in those scenarios you want to impress with something that identifies a problem then follow it up by a solution that you offer. You are trying to convey a short message in about 20-25 seconds max. So when you are meeting someone new at a party or social setting and the goal is gaining a new friend then you might say you love meeting new people and learning about them.

If the goal is to network or create a business relationship, then think about the service or product you would love this person to know about. Identify the problem(s) it solves and how you can help and go from there. You need to sell yourself before you sell anything else.

94.   DOOR-TO-DOOR

You want to get to the next level in your motivation and get out of your usual comfort zone? If you have just recently moved into your neighborhood it's the perfect time to do this. If you have lived there for years you could do this and be that much more motivated.

Many people when moving into a new house or apartment might go introduce themselves to the people that live directly next door so just one or two houses. I'm suggesting do the entire street and even include some businesses you plan to frequent too.

This will motivate you each time you leave one house to go to the next. What do you think the people at the other houses will think? Some might think you're crazy but most will be glad you came by and some might wonder why they never did that too. The next time you pass them on the street or see them in the grocery store you can say hello. Start building long lasting relationships and friendships now instead of chance meetings and realize you've lived on the same street for years and had never spoken.

95.   THE WEATHER

It has been said that if the weather never changed and stayed the same no one would know how to start a conversation or fill up some small talk. There are so many other things to talk about. Now I'd keep religion and politics at bay in the beginning but most people love to talk about themselves so I suggest that you ask some questions first.

Remember the five 'W's and the one 'H'. Who, what, where, when, why and how. You are at a social event so you may ask these six questions using our five Ws and one H. Who do you work for? What do you do in your spare time? When did you get into your job field? Why did you choose the neighborhood you live in? How do you know the host of the party?

You can still use the weather as the starting point but I'd change it up. Instead of "Cold enough for ya?" ask "What foods do you like to eat during cold weather like this?" or "What winter activities do you enjoy this time of year?" Instead of "I hate the rain!" Try "I bet we'll see a difference in our lawns and gardens after this rain. What things do you have in your garden?" or "What indoor things do you do when it's raining for this long?" Change your question/statement to something more positive and use open ended questions that require more than a yes or no to create great conversations.

Meeting new people and experiencing new situations will help with your motivation and inspire you to do more.

96.   ALWAYS A BEAUTIFUL DAY

This is a glass is half full kind of thinking and being more positive each day. I'm using this example as a metaphor for many topics.

Every day is beautiful no matter how much it is raining or snowing or even how windy it is. Look for reasons as to why something is that way and see it's benefits. I do a lot of driving and I don't like snow on those days but I know somebody might be looking at the snow from their window as I drive by and think how beautiful it is and they'd be correct. I don't ski but many people do and they likely get excited when a storm is coming.

Windy days are a kite's best friend and not just a day that makes you lose your hat. Rainy days are great for the flowers and the birds love the worms that come out of the ground on those days. I'm sure you see my point by now. Look at every day the same. With an open mind. My point is not all weather related either.

Look at every person, every situation, event, job or anything with a positive light and understand that there is a reason why someone or something is the way that they/it are. Look for the wonder and magnificence in the world around you. Soon, with a positive outlook, every storm will have a rainbow to look forward to.

97. POSITIVE REMINDERS

Keep positive reminders around you at all times. You should be surrounded by your favorite motivational or spiritual quotes. Keep books on the topic close at hand and keep various audio recordings near you when you commute or exercise.

Only positive reminders should be tolerated around you. Pictures of loved ones, positive or inspirational quotes by you or your friends, celebrities, your favorite authors, pictures of things you are working towards as part of your goals and items that have a spiritual connection for you should always be around to help motivate you and keep you from reverting back to your old unmotivated and negative self.

Even if you aren't religious in the least I would still recommend going to a place of worship occasionally as it is full of positive people with positive outlooks. Give it a try.

You will know that you have enough positive reminders when people come to your cubicle, office, home, car or just be in your space and it starts to rub off on them. When these people start getting motivated, inspired and become more positive than you, that's when you know you have enough reminders. In my Motivated Planner (details at the end of the book) it has quotes from this book for each day to keep you motivated at all times. It has areas to enter your goals and positive influencers for the day. Plus it has, instead of a vision board, it has vision pages. Somewhere you can put your constant reminders of your goals.

98.   You Can't Because You Haven't

Many people might be tempted when presented with the perceived impossible to say they can't do it. Remember, when you simply change the way to think or talk about different challenges, the way you identify them will transform your thoughts to more positive ones. You will think you can do the particular challenging task because you can do it.

Change "I can't" to "I haven't yet". Perhaps you were scared to even try something like public speaking so change that to "I haven't" because you haven't tried it. Perhaps you have tried but fell short like hitting your target weight but you've had some setbacks. In this example you would say "I haven't, yet" but you will.

You don't want to be the child that says you don't like broccoli but have never even tried it! How do you know you don't like it if you've never tried it? Perhaps it wasn't prepared the way you like it so you should also try it several different times before you put any kind of label on it.

99.   ALWAYS BE GRATEFUL

Another phase for this is to 'be in an attitude of gratitude'. The concept is an important one. When you write your goals down I also want you to add one thing you are grateful for that day or the previous day (depending on what time you write your goals down) so you can be motivated to be more grateful no matter how small it might be. My motivated planner also has areas to write in my daily gratitudes.

My wife and I have what we call a family blessings jar on our kitchen counter that we can see every time we are in the kitchen. Each day we write something on a slip of paper. We put the date on it with one or two sentences about what in that day made us grateful. Then January 1st each year my wife reads each one while my two sons and I sit at the kitchen table listening and telling stories about many of the blessings. It has become a tradition we look forward to doing.

When you have gratitude for even the little things it will help you look for more and more things to be grateful for and things that perhaps you took for granted. I'm going to say that I'm very grateful for you the reader for getting my book and I hope you feel more motivated after you read it. Perhaps you will have appreciation for me the author or if it was a gift – the person who gave it to you or for yourself for coming across it. Take a moment now to think about something that happened today or yesterday that you are grateful for and write it down on your Planner.

100. TAKE JUST ENOUGH TIME OFF

If you need time off, that's fine. However, only take enough to fulfill you. Have you ever taken more time than you usually do off? One of two things usually happen: you either can't wait to get back to work and your routine because the vacation was too relaxing and you felt lazy or you did too much and you're looking to do less back at work.

If you need time off, then take it. Don't whine all the time saying you need a holiday or be one of those people who count down to the weekend or always put TGIF on social media. That acronym should stand for 'Today's Goal I Forgot' because you were more focused on time off and didn't focus or care about your goal(s) for today. With all the '20 second vacation' and fill your calendar type rules you might have thought this rule was some sarcastic rule meant to kick you in the butt to get back at it. It is and it isn't. Take just enough time off and then get back to it.

101. TAKE IT TO THE NEXT LEVEL

Every product or service that has succeeded and done really well was taken to the next level by focused employees and motivated management. Why was that restaurant so successful? Why did that technology company take off? Why did your co-worker get a promotion? Because in every case they brought it to the next level. They gained momentum as people took notice.

Now think about everything you do. From your career to your family and everything in-between. Think about how you can bring it all to the next level. First think about what the next level is. If it's your job, then it isn't staying late one night because you were a team player and felt like you kicked it up a notch. There is a laundry list of things you could and should do to get a promotion and it doesn't mean just one thing or most things its everything. Like poker, all in or fold them. Teeth and claws or tuck your tail between your legs and go home. It must be all in or nothing.

When you aren't satisfied with goodness and only want greatness then you are on the right track. If you truly want more inspiration than you know what to do with, look at every nook and cranny of your life and bring it all to the next level.

102. THE NAPPING RULE

I've talked about the 20 second vacation to give you a little boost but sometimes that doesn't cut it. Sometimes we all need a little nap. They say the ideal amount of time for a nap is about 15-20 minutes so don't take your pants off and grab your teddy bear for a long time. If you sleep longer you will be more tired or it will take you longer to shake the drowsiness.

Some of the most successful business owners and executives take a nap in the afternoon. So set an alarm (or two!) and lay on the couch, on top of the bed covers or in a comfortable chair and take a nap if you think it will help you become more productive and sharp for the rest of the day. Power nap to re-charge your mind and body for greater overall success and motivation.

103. EXCEED YOUR POTENTIAL

Exceed your potential and not what someone or society says you can only do. We have all seen really successful people still working really hard and pushing themselves to do more. It's because they are exceeding their potential. Your potential far exceeds what you've been told you can do. Set your goals higher than what you think is the norm. Set your goals higher than you even think is possible.

You know deep down what you are capable of, so now increase it and challenge yourself to push beyond what is comfortable. Work to your potential and not some statistic you saw on television or some quota your sales manager gave you or what you were told your 'target weight' is. Keep pushing to your potential and then keep pushing. You and I both know you can do it.

104. WHAT YOU LIKE ABOUT YOUR CURRENT SITUATION

No matter what your job is or how your marriage is, there must be at least one thing that is positive. You need to write at least one thing in each area of your life that you enjoy or like. It's important when trying to make any kind of change that you are aware there is still some good and that perhaps a 100% change isn't necessary.

If you really dislike your job (did you notice, I didn't say hate?) think about the few things you do like. Focus on the positive and don't dwell on the negative. This will help you until you do find a new job or perhaps realize the current one isn't so bad. Maybe you enjoy working with a particular co-worker or client or performing a specific task or even the brand is one you have always admired.

This process is to get you always in the right frame of mind and to seek out the positive in most situations. If you get in that habit, then you'll start seeing the brighter picture no matter how dark everyone else's view is.

105. WRITE A DAILY TO-DO LIST

It is important to write goals everyday but you won't get to your goal(s) without a map. You will find your way easier when you write a daily to-do list to get it all done. It will keep you on track and focused. Keep referring to your to-do list and your goals throughout the day.

Nothing keeps you more focused than actually putting pen to paper, and not typing it on your phone or tablet. You can put it in those things too but when you write it down it's like you are committing to it as it gives it more meaning. The pen is truly mightier than the sword. After you have completed each task, there is a sense of satisfaction when you physically cross it off or put a check mark beside it.

Your plan of action should include your daily tasks and the things you need to do to hit your goals each day. It is so very important that you write these 15 minute blocks that we talked about each and every day. Don't forget to write down a time that you will be writing your goals and to-do list tomorrow to keep your schedule tight and jam packed with excitement.

106. DOCUMENT YOUR SUCCESSES

Every day you will be writing down your goals, targets, big ideas and other things in your Motivated Planner. Once you achieve certain accomplishments you need to write it down and document it. You'll want to look back at them later to give you an extra push when you're having a particularly tough day. When you review them you will remember how each one was challenging yet you persevered and achieved your goal. If you did it then, you can do it now. That's why there is a section each day in the Motivated Planner to put your accomplishments.

Where are you making improvements? Where are your successes? What did you win at and how did you win at it? Most people remember big wins in their life but when you write small and medium ones down too and refer back to it from time to time, watch how much more motivated you become. You will start seeking out similar situations because you know you crushed it the last time you came across this task or problem.

You have to start paying attention to all these small, medium and giant successes. If you stop paying attention to them, they may stop paying attention to you. In fact, you may stop having them altogether. Write them down and talk about all of your successes.

107. EVERY MORNING WRITE YOUR GOALS

Every morning you wake up write your goals down. You need to write your goals down as soon as your feet hit the floor. Try and do it before you even use the washroom or get out of bed. Keep a pen and paper beside your bed. It's best to write it in your planner so you continually see it throughout the day.

This isn't to be confused with your daily tasks or to-do list. These are the goals that are the very reason you get up early each morning. These goals should inspire you to be the very best that day. You have to stay motivated on YOUR goals and targets because if you aren't you will be helping others reach their goals and not yours. If you write them every morning, you are halfway there.

108. EVERY EVENING WRITE YOUR GOALS

Now that you have written them at the beginning of your day, you now need to write them towards the end of your day too. These goals could be long term goals. If you need a system, that's fine. Perhaps you write daily goals in the morning and long term in the evening. However you do it, it is important to write your goals twice a day.

Write where you want to be in a month, a year or five years. What is your 10-year goal? What do you want your life to look like in 20 years?

You want to wake up thinking about your goals and go to sleep thinking about them. If you have a little trouble falling asleep after you write them, that's fantastic, you know it's working then because your goals should excite you.

109. GARBAGE IN, GARBAGE OUT

Remember everything we've talked about. You want to reduce all negativity in your life because you bring it in and you're more likely to spew it out too. Eat lots of things that aren't good for you, then your body will give off negative energy by not having the fuel to get through your day. You will not have that drive and motivation you need to succeed.

Garbage is all the negative stuff I've talked about that you don't want or need in your life. You bring that garbage in your life and you can rest assured you will be joining in on the negative downward spiral that is the unmotivated, negative person. In this case, recycling is bad. Throw it all out.

110. STAND TALL

It doesn't matter if you are standing or sitting, you must do it straight. Stand tall and straight. Don't slouch in your chair. When you stand tall and puff out your chest a little, square up your shoulders and keep your head up you not only scream to the world you are a confident person but you also tell yourself. That alone can motivate you a lot.

When you see someone hunched over you think the person isn't comfortable in their surroundings or unhealthy or not self-assured. However, more often than not I find this more true for the actual person. They start feeling bad about themselves.

So stand tall and watch your motivation and self-confidence stand taller. When you do this you will feel like you are up for any challenge or any goal that you set.

111. FIRM HANDSHAKE, WARM HUGS

In business a firm handshake can mean confidence or a strong leader. When meeting someone in a social setting it can also mean they are friendly, they like and respect you. To me a soft or "limp fish" handshake shows you don't care or lack the confidence in yourself or the other person.

Take extra effort when meeting new people or even the people you've already met. Shake hands with and start (or continue) to give firm handshakes to everyone in your life. As you shake hands look into the eyes of the other person to show you care about meeting them. You might even try focusing in on just one of the other persons' eyes. This will likely go unnoticed consciously but sub-consciously it will exude self-confidence.

When the time is right and the situation dictates it, nothing says you care more than giving a warm hug no matter what gender you are or the other person. This will make you feel good and it will likely make the other person feel good. You'll be motivated to give and receive more due to the positive feelings it produces. Hug someone today.

112. BE DIFFERENT

Be different from the norm and everyone else who is unmotivated, looking for shortcuts and just going through the paces of everyday life. Those people are alive but they aren't living and they are definitely not full of life.

This book has given you many different ways to get motivated and stay motivated. One way is to stand out and be noticed by being different. Everyone's definition of different varies. However, to excel in your life and reach your goals is often different. Spending time with seniors at a center is different. Writing your goals twice a day, over 700 times a year is different. Walking up to a perfect stranger to strike up a conversation to make a new friend is different.

Actions speak louder than words so do more rather than telling. Different doesn't has to be an outrageous outfit, crazy hairstyle or listen to 'weird' music but if you like to do that and especially if it motivates you to be different every day then more power to you. Go for it. Again, I'm not talking about some trick with some attention grabber.

Being different shouldn't mean you are the target of bullies or eye rolling. It needs to be celebrated. Being different means you are a role model, a motivator, a teacher, one that inspires and seeks positive change. Think about all of history's characters who left a positive long-lasting transformation and helped shape the world we are in today. All of them were given the label of a person who is different and stood out among the rest.

Being different can also make you memorable and that's what you want. Don't do what everyone else is doing because that's what everyone else is doing. Set yourself apart from everyone by doing many of the things we've already talked about. Go above and beyond, always help others, constantly strive to be the very best and enjoy every second that you're doing it.

Be different by your actions. Be set apart from others. Friends, family and co-workers will say things like "You're different from the rest" because you are always looking for ways to help others and thus it helps to motivate you and you will reach your own goals faster.

113. VOLUNTEER IN YOUR COMMUNITY

When you help someone out it empowers you to do even more. Even something as simple as holding a door open for someone can feel good. Now power it up by volunteering in your community. It is an amazing feeling. You may also choose to become a big brother or big sister and mentor a young person. How about coaching a kid's sports team? Have you ever thought of becoming a local politician and serving your community as a counselor or other position?

Whatever the capacity, lending your time will inspire you and others around you to do more and help others. Set some time aside each month to volunteer and make a difference in your city.

Start off small and donate an hour or two once a month and see if you can increase it in a month or two. Perhaps raise money for charity or help at a charity event. Doing any of these things will inspire you to look for other areas you can lend a hand. Help and be inspired.

114. DONATE

If you donate your time, that's fantastic. If you felt inspired and more motivated that's wonderful. Now, if you can, donate your money, old clothes, your kid's old toys or nonperishable food that's even better. Donate different things and donate often.

This is usually another instant gratification motivator. Once you donate, even a few dollars, it can do wonders for your feeling of self-worth. Look to donate at least once a month to a charity, church, hospital or other worthy cause. Donate loose change at the donation boxes at stores or other places.

Donate to feel more motivated. Think about where you donate and where the money goes to help so many different people. Perhaps you have a charity that you identify with because you were personally affected by a certain disease that you or a loved one got. You may want to concentrate and put all of your focus on it. It doesn't matter how much or to what organization. You will feel so good doing it and it will benefit both you and the organization or charity.

115. START A FOUNDATION OR NON-PROFIT

If you were really inspired by the previous two rules, then perhaps you will really get inspired to take it to the next level and start your own foundation or nonprofit.

If it's a specific niche charity that you found isn't already covered by some other charity or a nonprofit to help some area of your community that is great and I encourage it. Being at the helm of something like that is a powerful motivator. You will more than likely help to inspire and motivate others to possibly do the same.

116. BUILD YOUR LEGACY

Many of the things I've talked about in this book. Especially the previous one will build your legacy. Knowing that you will leave a legacy is a very powerful motivator. Many of us have kids and they are an extension of us and part of you will live on in them long after you die.

There are many other ways to build your legacy so what you do now will live on beyond the grave. Starting a foundation or nonprofit are just two examples.

The other obvious one is what you are reading. A book. Think about what you know, your job, your hobby, your passion, something your parents or grandparents taught you. Think of a niche topic and write a short book about it. You likely won't get rich on it but it will live on past you. I wrote this book in hopes of motivating others as I wasn't so motivated at different times in my life. I actually became so much more motivated even from when I decided to write the book versus when I finished it.

One other thing you could do is start a blog, vlog or get interviewed by print or digital media. All those outlets will forever document your thoughts and ideas. When you build your legacy you will get an unmatched sense of motivation, determination and a powerful sense of purpose.

117. KIDS AND ANIMALS

I was hesitant about putting this one in the book. There are people that dislike one or both of these so if you're that person then please skip to the next one.

Spending time with your children (or other people's children) and teaching them something or giving them inspiration can give you the same. I encourage you, if you are not a parent, uncle or aunt to become a big brother or big sister to a young person and become their mentor to help the next generation of young people.

As for animals, I may not get motivated or inspired being around a dog, cat or other animal but it's the good positive feeling when you bond with an animal that you take care of or play with or even just sit on the couch and pet. Don't knock this until you have done it. It will build a connection when the animal responds to you and thus make you feel great. Try it.

118.   READ, LISTEN AND REPEAT

How committed to change are you? Do you really want to get motivated? Do you want to stay motivated? If this book is your first one on the subject or the 100th you can't read it just once.

If you read a book I suggest getting the audio book, if you started listening to an audio book I suggest getting the book. When I say book I mean both the physical printed book and the Ebook. There are advantages and disadvantages to both so get the pair, especially if you found it at all helpful. Read and listen to each book more than once and take notes if necessary.

You want to memorize the content like you're about to be tested on it. If you have made a commitment to yourself to get motivated, then go all in and do it! Don't do it half-assed or you will only see very little change if you see any change at all.

119. GET OUT!

It is necessary if you want to get motivated to get out of the house and get out often. When you stay in your house or apartment you are breathing in stale air and getting little to no sunshine. Lack of fresh air and sunshine will kill your inspiration. Get out and take a walk, exercise, go to the library or mall for a change of scenery but nothing beats sunshine and fresh air.

You also need to get out of your comfort zone in a big way so look to do that in every scenario. Get out of the mundane and get into inspiration.

120. WALK A MILE IN SOMEONE ELSE'S SHOES

Having compassion and empathy are amazing traits to have. Once you know what it feels like to walk in another's shoes, as the saying goes, then it will motivate you to want to help more.

By helping I mean doing things such as volunteering in your community, helping a friend, raise money for charity, join a group or assisting an elderly neighbor. Get involved and it will benefit you and the person you are helping. Start small by mowing the lawn or shoveling the driveway of an older person you know or know of. You might not even have ever spoken to this person and you both have lived on the same street for years. It doesn't matter, that's the past.

121. NEVER WISH YOU COULD LIVE SOMEONE ELSE'S LIFE

If you wish you could have someone else's life or be them, then stop. Perhaps it's a singer, actor or even a friend or neighbor whose life you envy. First of all, it's very unhealthy.

It is all or nothing. The next time you have that thought take a moment and think about making the entire swap. Are you really willing to give up everything you have? Will you trade your kids, spouse, parents, sibling, friends and memories? Will you give up and trade all that for the other person's wealth, fame, talents or social status? Remember, you must also take all of their life so everything you don't know and their problems.

Once you consider that you'll likely change your mind. It's like the saying "The grass is always greener on the other side." Build your own life and successes. Build strength and character from your so called failures and become a better person than the people you once wanted to be.

122. REMEMBER TO BREATHE

Sometimes in life we feel anxious. It can be social settings like a party or wedding. It can be for business for a meeting or it can be in front of audience, no matter what size. It those times it might be so anxious for you that it sucks out your motivation to the point of you stepping back and wondering if you even want to do it. These are the times you need to remember to breath.

You might be thinking, do I really need to remember to breathe? You do and especially in certain times. Place your hand right now just below your chest and above your stomach in the center. Now take a deep breath through your nose and out your mouth. Really fill your lungs. Now say hello to your diaphragm.

In times of uncertainty when you get the first signs that you are anxious but before any motivation starts to leave you, remember to breathe. Three very deep and controlled breaths in through your nose and out through the mouth should be enough to get you off the ledge of the unmotivated cliff.

123. GO NOW

Don't put it off for another second. I'm talking about starting to get motivated and everything else important in your life that up to now you have put off and procrastinated about doing. Don't put off a single thing from now on. Jump in with both feet and do everything and then do a little more.

Soon if not already there are tasks that would normally have taken the old you triple the amount of time, assuming you even completed them. Go now and do what you have always wanted. Get super motivated and stay motivated.

CONCLUSION

I hope you have learned something from this book. If you are reading this part, then I really hope you have read everything before these words. If you have, then congratulations! I'm so happy for you because getting motivated is now as easy as 1-2-3. I hope you will be super motivated.

Every 'rule' or 'way' in How to Get Motivated - 123 Ways to Get AND Stay Motivated has been carefully thought of to motivate as many people as it can. Remember what I said at the very beginning; motivation is like taking a bath or shower. It has been done every day because this feeling won't last more than a day at first. You need to repeat it tomorrow, the next day and so on. Don't forget to read it again and again. Get the ebook and/or print book, audio book and use the Motivating Planner each day. It's about not just having a few moments of inspiration a few times a week but constantly having a motivational boost always at your fingertips to power through your day, every day.

Don't be afraid to ask for help via friends, family or even more books like this and others. There is so much help out there to help in all areas of motivation. If you are feeling lower than being unmotivated and more depressed, please seek professional help. Know that you are not alone in your struggle and life is meant to be enjoyed and I plead with you to get help. Often the help you need is just a click or call away.

How to Get Motivated and STAY Motivated

Sometimes being motivated means just taking control and not feeling so overwhelmed. Document your goals and look at them every single day. It's so important that's why I developed the Motivated Planner. Use it to plan your day, your goals and life all well getting and staying motivated. The name means two things; the first is that it will help you stay motivated throughout your day. The second is what you will become. You will become a motivated planner. You will be motivated as you plan your day and during your day.

The Motivated Planner is a daily planner that I have come up with using the very concepts and techniques within this book to help you plan your day, week and month. Remember to keep it filled to stay motivated throughout your day. It even has quotes from the book, spots for your own quotes, your goals, your successes and much more. Get the planner at www.123ways.com

Can you please do a favor for me? Would you please take a moment and write a review for this book? If you got this on a site that allows for reviews, please leave one for me. As a thank you head over to Be Super Motivated (link below) to pick up your free gift as my thanks!

To sign up for advance notices or to get a free chapter of the audio and/or ebook, or events such as book signings go to www.123ways.com If you want me to speak at your event or at your company on motivation please contact me. Please go to www.123ways.com/contact

I would also love to hear all about your successes and breakthroughs as so I can share them with others and perhaps help them. Let's connect. Let's motivate. Let's be motivated. Let's get motivated!

"If you aren't motivated, then nothing else matters, does it?" – Kevin A MacKenzie

How to Get Motivated and STAY Motivated

Manufactured by Amazon.ca
Bolton, ON